PLANNING YOUR ESCAPE

PLANNING YOUR ESCAPE

STRATEGY SECRETS *to* MAKE YOU *an* ESCAPE ROOM SUPERSTAR

L.E. HALL

TILLER PRESS

New York   London   Toronto   Sydney   New Delhi

TILLER PRESS

An Imprint of Simon & Schuster, Inc.
1230 Avenue of the Americas
New York, NY 10020

First Tiller Press trade paperback edition August 2021

TILLER PRESS and colophon are trademarks of Simon & Schuster, Inc.

For information about special discounts for bulk purchases,
please contact Simon & Schuster Special Sales at 1-866-506-1949
or business@simonandschuster.com.

The Simon & Schuster Speakers Bureau can bring authors to your live event. For more information or to book an event, contact the Simon & Schuster Speakers Bureau at 1-866-248-3049 or visit our website at www.simonspeakers.com.

Interior design by Davina Mock-Maniscalco

Manufactured in the United States of America

1 3 5 7 9 10 8 6 4 2

Library of Congress Cataloging-in-Publication Data has been applied for.

ISBN 978-1-9821-4034-2
ISBN 978-1-9821-4035-9 (ebook)

For Jey, my partner in puzzles and in life

CONTENTS

Contents

PART 1

WELCOME TO THE WORLD OF ESCAPE ROOMS

Imagine this: You stand shoulder to shoulder with seven other people in a little group. You're facing a closed office door. Your assignment: to get through that door, no matter what's stopping you.

And at the moment, what's stopping you is a very stubborn secretary.

The secretary stands firm against your pleas. This is the office of a vital person in the communications office, she tells you, and she can't just let you in.

Unless, she adds with a knowing wink, you happen to have something you can trade for her to look the other way.

You confer with your friends. One of your teammates hands the woman a set of food-ration coupons, usable in the made-up country of Argovia.

The secretary is delighted with the bribe. She thanks you profusely, saying this will more than cover her midday meal and that she'll be back in an hour—and please, don't break anything.

She holds the office door open as your group files in, closing it behind you with a firm *click*.

Inside the room, the lights are dim. The space is filled with large, boxy shapes.

You pause to let your eyes adjust to the darkness. There's a clunking sound, like a big machine whirring to life, and an electric buzz fills the room as the lights turn on, one by one. You and your friends look around excitedly to see what you're dealing with.

You find yourself standing in the office of a bureaucrat, obviously a cog in some type of dystopian government machine. There are big propaganda posters on the walls; books on a shelf locked behind a grille; a typewriter with strange letters on its keys.

On the wall, a timer blinks on: sixty minutes. It begins counting down.

The game is on.

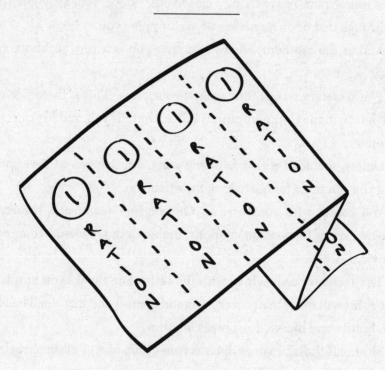

A paper prop from the Spark of Resistance escape room

This is the scenario for Spark of Resistance, an escape room that I opened with five friends in 2014 in Portland, Oregon.

In the story, the players were a team of spies, activated for a secret mission: to infiltrate a double agent's office.

"Our double agent has missed a vital check-in, and we fear that something has happened to them. We need you and your special puzzle-solving skills to investigate the double agent's office and figure out where they've gone."

Over the span of sixty minutes, players explored the office, met up with the double agent, were betrayed when the agent escaped the building without them, and then freed themselves—but only if they completed all the puzzles in time, of course.

It was the first escape room in the state and one of the first in the Pacific Northwest. We learned a lot from designing and building it and even more from watching thousands of people play it.

Is a couple good at communicating with each other? Is a work team well synchronized? Does a family have a strong dynamic? Drop them in an escape room, close the door, hit the timer, and find out.

Escape rooms are the perfect exercises in communicating, assessing information, and making decisions quickly. As such, every player has their strengths and weaknesses.

What this book aims to do is help you identify yours—and use that knowledge to slay every room you encounter. (With your similarly armed friends, of course!) In fact, you can use the tools in this book to improve not only your escape room game but also your chances of solving any puzzle—because, as you'll learn, they all operate from the same set of principles.

The makers and players of immersive puzzle games come from many different backgrounds. Still, one thing we all have in common is a sense of curiosity and a willingness to challenge ourselves.

I design escape rooms and puzzle games for a living, and while it's been a long, meandering road to this point, I have definitely always loved mysteries.

I grew up reading about kid detectives like Nancy Drew and Encyclopedia Brown, and I loved stories about strange events and hidden treasures, like Graeme Base's children's book *The Eleventh Hour*.

In college, I discovered the interactive, live Internet games called ARGs, or alternate reality games. (In fact, that's how I met my partner, who created the first ARG I ever played.) ARGs play out across the web, with codes hidden in websites, phone numbers leading to live actors, and, sometimes, actual buried treasure—all reached by solving puzzles.

I was officially hooked.

When we moved to Portland, we were welcomed by someone I knew through the ARG community forums but had never met in person. He introduced us to a monthly puzzle-solving event called Puzzled Pint. Every second Tuesday of the month, people gather in bars and restaurants to solve themed puzzles on paper alongside their friends.

With Puzzled Pint, I honed my skills and started thinking of myself as a "puzzler" for the first time. I also met an amazing group of people with a similarly deep interest in this admittedly nerdy pursuit. When we heard that an escape room had opened in a nearby state, we immediately hit the road.

I'd never seen anything like it: it was all the stuff I loved from detective stories and puzzle games, but life-size—a room with objects, padlocks, and clues that you could actually touch.

On the drive back, we were ecstatic. This medium's incredible potential was already clear: escape rooms were like live, participatory theater crossed with video games.

"Let's make one," we said. "How hard can it be?" (Spoiler alert: very!)

After a lot of sweat and a little bit of blood and tears, we opened Spark of Resistance. And since then, we've been lucky to make many more exciting adventures for the curious at heart.

My goal with this book is to open up the world of escape rooms to as many new players as possible and give them the tools to succeed.

So let's start at the beginning. Whether you're an expert with hundreds of games under your belt or just an enthusiastic beginner, this book has something for everyone.

First, we'll explore how escape rooms came to exist. It's an incredible historical journey, from archaeological digs—who knew that escape rooms could be linked to ancient Mesopotamia?—to the latest and greatest in virtual-reality technology.

Because entertainment evolves along with people's ability to access it, it's also a story about how humans travel and gather together: first on foot, then by train, and now via the Internet.

Games are universal. Play is what links all humans (and even many animals) together: we share in feelings of joy and release, and play inspires us as teammates to create something greater than our individual selves.

Next, we'll learn how escape rooms work and how to solve them.

After that, I'll show you how to recognize different types of puzzles and ciphers and what to look out for with keys, padlocks, electromagnets, and more. You'll learn about how games are structured, what your game monitor is thinking, how hints work, and how to avoid red herrings.

And I'll teach you how to work well together as a team, with strategies for communication and empathy during gameplay.

Armed with this knowledge, you'll be able to tackle any escape room game, whether at home or on location, keep your team flowing, and solve puzzles like a pro.

Let's go, puzzlers!

CHAPTER 1

What Is an Escape Room?

Alone we can do so little. Together we can do so much.
—HELEN KELLER

What is an escape room? That's a great question, dear reader, and I'm glad you asked it.

Escape rooms are puzzle games* with a time limit,* set in a locked room,* played with a team,* in the real world.*

Let's start with the original escape rooms: real-world, interactive games.

In these rooms, you're going to be with a team of people, and you'll be shown into a decorated room of some kind, and when the door closes behind you, a timer will start and you'll have to solve as many puzzles as you can before it runs out.

"Solving puzzles with a timer running? This sounds like an elaborate form of torture," you may be saying. "Didn't I see a horror movie about this?"

As a person who has played many escape rooms, as well as someone

---

*Most of the time, anyway. Escape rooms can also be board games, paper-based games, or computer games played virtually. We'll discuss other types of escape rooms in a later part of this book.

who has created many games for other people to play, I can assure you: it is fun.

Really fun, actually! And no, we won't kill you (literally or figuratively) if you don't make it out in time, I promise.

More important, escape rooms are an awesome way to connect with friends, family, coworkers, or even strangers:

Like playing a board game, you're in person, spending time together.

Like playing sports, you're on a team, with everyone working to achieve the same goal.

Like playing a video game, you have to figure out the rules of the world and learn how to master them.

And like watching a movie, you're getting to see a cool story.

Truth be told, even if you don't win, it's still a good time, because other people are what make it fun. You enter the game as individuals and come out on the other side as a team. And, I hope, you experience a little bit of story magic along the way.

CHAPTER 2

Ancient History to the 1800s

We can only know where we're going if we know where we've been.
—MAYA ANGELOU

Escape rooms have an interesting history. They may seem like a new trend, but in truth, they're an extension of a long legacy of in-person entertainment.

Much of today's entertainment takes place on screens. The video game industry, for example, is worth hundreds of billions of dollars. One thing that sets escape rooms apart is that they're "embodied"— that is, they take place in a physical space, with other people present. In the cultural context of the video game age, anything that's successfully getting people to come together in the real world is worth a closer look.

We can trace the way escape rooms came to be part of this realm of embodied entertainment through the creation of entertainment venues like theme parks, the history of experimental theater, the development of computers and arcade games, and the introduction of game and puzzle vocabulary to the general public through game shows on TV.

Something that's always fascinated me about in-person entertainment is how it evolves alongside humanity's ability to travel and gather.

First of all, humans love to play! Always have, always will. Toys, dice, and game components have been found in archaeological dig sites all over the world, and the rules of some games, like Senet from ancient Egypt, have survived to this day. The Chinese game Go is 2,500 years old, and there's evidence that Mancala was played in Jordan around the year 6000 BC.

So when you see news articles about a "new fad" like board games or puzzle rooms, just remember that, in spirit, they're not so new. Rather, they're speaking to something ancient and familiar. What *is* new is how we access those games and who we play them with.

Back when entertainment and large gatherings were only accessible by foot, on horseback, or on a cart pulled by an ox, we saw epic events like the Olympics in Greece (776 BC through AD 260) and medieval fairs in twelfth-century Europe.

In the early 1800s, transportation underwent a major shift. People traveled around cities via horse-drawn trams and streetcars, and reached new places on steamships and ferries.

The more travel became possible, the more destinations appeared to travel *to*: pleasure gardens, world's-fair exhibitions of human innovation and invention, even trolley parks located at the end of streetcar lines (to make sure that people kept buying tickets on the weekends).

Whenever people can travel, entertainment follows.

PEOPLE AND PLAY

Pakistan, 2500s BC

Picture this scene: a city street with high brick walls and a small alley where children have gathered to play. Nearby are the bustling sounds of city life, rolling cart wheels and overheard conversations.

The children are crouching around a set of dice, taking turns rolling them and picking up short sticks. A small boy is playing with a clay figurine of a dog, moving it around on the ground. He makes it bark at a figurine of an ox, which rises up on its hind legs in response.

Nearby, another child sits on a step, concentrating hard.

He is holding a clay disk with raised ridges in a labyrinth pattern. Inside the channel created by the ridges is a clay marble. The child tilts the disk, gently adjusting the angles to roll the marble along. Suddenly the marble picks up speed, and the child quickly corrects the movement, tilting the disk in the other direction—but it's too much, too fast, and the marble bounces off, hitting the pavement below and rolling away.

One of the dice-playing children picks up the marble and hands it back to her friend without even looking up from her game.

This scene could take place in any city, at any time in history; these children and their games are instantly recognizable. But the scene I'm thinking of is set in Mohenjo-daro, a city in the Indus Valley, nearly five thousand years ago.

High in the Himalayan mountains, the Indus River flows toward the Arabian Sea. Over many years, it has carved out a valley. Nearly five thousand years ago, hundreds of thousands of people lived in 1,400 towns in what is now Pakistan and Northern India.

Mohenjo-daro was an incredible city, with urban development on the level of Rome, which wouldn't appear until a good 2,500 years later. It's laid out in a grid format, with multistory brick buildings and a complex sewer system that fed homes with fresh water and removed their waste. It's one of the first urban centers in human history.

No one has yet translated the Indus language, so we have to turn to an archaeologist's perspective to understand them as a people: What do the remains of their cities and the objects found there tell us about their interests, their families, their lives? What kind of people would live in these buildings and use these items?

As always, the most fascinating finds are the small details that reveal that, no matter how long ago these people lived, they were not really so different from you or me.

The excavation of Mohenjo-daro began in 1922 with its discovery by history professor R. D. Banerji, an officer of the Archaeological Survey of India, and paused around 1965 to preserve the structures from weathering due to exposure.

In that period, archaeologists uncovered wonderful artifacts, including a bronze statue of a young girl posing with an instantly recognizable teenage attitude, and a soapstone carving of an aristocratic, bearded man wearing ornamental head- and armbands and a decorative cloak over one shoulder.

But the smaller items that were found are equally revealing. There were a lot of terra-cotta artifacts, including many toys that look like they would barely survive being played with by today's children—so it's all the more remarkable that they've lasted 4,500 years.

There were little figures of oxen, including intact carts made from straw, and a small ram's head on a bird's body, with wheels on either side.

There were also lots of game markers and six-sided dice, exactly the same as you'd get in a game box today. And there were maze puzzles.

These maze puzzles are clay objects that look like small plates with raised ridges in a maze pattern, creating narrow channels. The idea is to set a marble in the maze channel, then tilt the plate to move the marble along without it dropping into another channel or falling off entirely. This type of dexterity game still exists today—I've played them. (They're hard!)

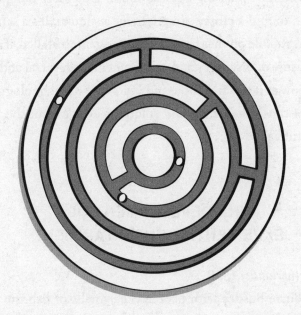

A wooden maze puzzle with small clay balls. Similar puzzles were found during the excavation of Mohenjo-daro.

In fact, this puzzle style caused a stir in 1889, when it was reinvented and produced by toymaker Charles Martin Crandall.

His version of the game, dubbed Pigs in Clover, was made of wood and paper, with the marbles representing pigs being driven into a pen in the center. It was an instant hit. The *Waverly Free Press* wrote about it at the time: "Of course you've seen the new puzzle, 'Pigs in Clover.' It is astonishing how quick that toy has captured the city."[1]

The public craving for Pigs in Clover lasted for several months, and the newspaper wrote that it was "to be found on the oars and the ferryboats, in counting-rooms and law offices, in restaurants and in bar rooms. It is offered for sale on every street corner," and had even "invaded the United States Senate chamber." A later article in the same paper reported that two million units had been sold within a year.[2]

The passion for puzzling persists today. Open any newspaper and you're bound to find a crossword puzzle or a sudoku. It's a safe bet that most people's mobile phones have at least one game installed, if not many.

The pleasure of discovery and achievement is universal and timeless, as relevant now as it was five thousand years ago. As technology changes, the nature of those challenges and solutions evolves, but the feeling of delight is identical.

THE DEVELOPMENT OF EXPERIENTIAL ENTERTAINMENT

Southern Netherlands, 1550

The town square bustles with people. The smells of fish, smoke, beer, and gingerbread waft through the air. There's noise everywhere: music, laughter, excited chatter.

In a pub nearby, people dance merrily. Stalls outside sell gingerbread in the shape of flowers, birds, and armor. Nearby, a woman cooks waffles on an iron over a fire, while at another stall, a woman chops fish.

Puppets dance and perform in the window of a small booth as tourists look on, sitting side by side with market vendors still wearing their aprons and pretty young girls giggling together.

People wear all sorts of costumes: the colorful motley of a jester, masks, and funny hats. One man has even tied waffles to his head.

A procession of revelers makes its way between the buildings and toward the square. Down the road, a child stuffs his mouth with a pancake as he runs to find a good spot to watch the parade. As he wedges himself in among the crowd, an egg lands at his feet.

With a shriek, he squints up at the buildings nearby. A lady standing on a balcony laughs and waves, an egg in her other hand, ready to toss upon another unsuspecting pedestrian.

The people shuffle to either side of the narrow passage to make way for the procession.

People in animal masks and brightly colored clothes gambol and dance in front of carts filled with people making music and singing. One man plays a flute; another raps a drum, keeping time.

A man in a mask and cape makes noise with a straw driven through a skin drawn taut over the mouth of a clay pot as a costumed figure with a round belly and pot on their head strums a stringed lute.

In the crowd, a man bangs a wooden spoon on a pot, adding to the clamor.

This is a community festival in the 1550s, a time when people of shared towns and villages came together to celebrate the changing of the seasons and to indulge in frivolity and fun.

These major events were precursors to celebrations and gatherings that we hold to this day. The path to contemporary entertainment like theme parks begins here, with roots in festivals in ancient and medieval times.

FOOT TRAFFIC

For most of human existence, travel was limited to where we could go on foot; where we could get on the back of a horse, ox, or donkey; and where we could get via ship . . . at least until the boat lands, at which point, we're back on foot or on top of an animal. Travel was often dangerous, time-consuming, and laborious. Yet throughout human history, there have been festivals, fairs, and sports competitions.

These events were what we would call liminal, a word that describes transitions or boundaries between spaces, both real or imagined, such as the space between life and death. There is a line drawn around liminal events, metaphorically (and sometimes literally). These events exist only for a specific amount of time, in a specific space, and then disperse.

Games, incidentally, are also liminal: people come together to play, they understand the new rules of the temporary situation, they complete the game, and the temporary situation ends, with the understanding that rules of the world now return to normal.

In ancient times, these liminal spaces often represented a time when political grudges were put on hold, such as when Olympic athletes were granted safe passage to travel to the games even if the countries between were warring. In medieval times, fairs and festivals were a chance for structures of power to be temporarily reversed, with events like the crowning of the fool.

When these events ended, life returned to normal, though sometimes people walked away changed, having gained new knowledge and new experiences.

The Ancient Olympics

The ancient games were held from 776 BC through AD 260 in Olympia, near the western coast of the Peloponnese peninsula of southern Greece. Olympia was known for its magnificent temples to Zeus and Hera, making it a fitting location for an event to honor the twelve gods.

Citizens traveled from as far away as modern-day Spain and Turkey to participate, and an "Olympic truce" was put in place to allow competitors and spectators safe passage.[3]

Olympia was an area of about a square kilometer, surrounded on three sides by a wall that denoted its status as a sacred space. Inside the wall were temples of Zeus and Hera and administrative buildings for the ancient games. Outside the wall were the stadium, hippodrome, athlete baths, and hotels for visitors.

According to Pausanias, a Greek traveler in the second century AD, there were statues along the path to the stadium commemorating athletes who won races, as well as a sort of "avenue of shame" with statues of athletes who were caught cheating or accepting bribes.

As the Romans conquered Greece, the prominence of the Olympic Games declined. When Christianity was declared the official religion of the Roman Empire, they were banned in AD 393 as pagan festivals by Emperor Theodosius.

The Olympics as we know them today were revived in 1896, and while the games don't have the same religious connotations as their predecessor, they still represent the original ideal of unity between mind, body, and will, and the coming together of many nations.

Some pagan elements remain, however, such as the symbolic lighting of the torch and its relay, introduced by the Third Reich in 1936. At Olympia, Greece, the torch is lit using a parabolic mirror to focus the rays of the sun, representing the flame of Zeus's altar. The torch is then carried by a series of people to the site of the Olympic games.[4]

Fairs and Festivals

Fairs and festivals were a major part of medieval European citizens' lives, and wow, did they love to party.

In England during the twelfth century, people had to seek permission from their local political and religious bodies to gather together in person. Towns would receive charters to hold fairs, which were chances for merchants to trade their wares and for people to let loose in between strict religious observances.

The opportunity to make money was enticing for everyone involved. Merchants could reach many customers at once. The local nobles and church of the town would make a profit from sales. And from that income, they would pay taxes benefitting the Crown, who had given the charter.

In ancient Italy and Greece, polytheists held feasts and celebrations to mark the changing of the seasons, indicated by the relationship of the sun's position to the earth. The solstices happen in June (summer solstice) and December (winter solstice), marking the shortest and longest days of the year. The spring and fall equinoxes happen in March (vernal equinox) and September (autumnal equinox), marking days and nights of equal length.

In Rome, there were many events set around the winter solstice, including raucous multiweek feasts honoring Saturn and celebrations of the birth of the sun god Sol Invictus featuring games and chariot racing. As Christianity rose in Rome, between the second and fourth centuries AD scholars debated and eventually settled on the date of the birth of Jesus Christ as December 25.

Although the exact history is unclear, it appears that over the following centuries, solstice-related partying merged with the more austere "Christ's Mass," setting the scene for the celebration of Christmas that's known today.

Until the establishment and rise of Christmas, the biggest ecclesiastical event was Easter, an event around the spring equinox. The period before Easter is known as Lent, a symbolic forty-day period of fasting and repentance.

And before that fast is a celebratory period known as Carnival, from the Late Latin *carne levare*, or "remove meat," as adherents abstain from meat. (This was also a convenient way to help people use up the remainder of the food they had stored over the winter.)

Carne can also refer to the flesh of the body, as people indulged in feasting and frivolity before the long period of religious piety resumed.

They listened to music, ate, drank, danced, attended parades, played sports and games, watched plays, told stories, and, of course, came decked out in their most special, brightly colored clothes. (One person visiting a fair in Naples wrote of the "laced jacket and flame-colored stockings" and "enormous" buckles worn by commoners.[5])

There were also important symbolic rituals attached to these events. Carnival was a way to turn the world upside down in a sanctioned and temporary way. It was a chance to use farce and irreverence to recognize, comment upon, and critique the frustrations as well as the pleasures of their difficult lives.

Events representing the symbolic upending of social order included servants giving orders to their masters, laypeople delivering sermons, and the mock crowning of a Carnival king, whose rise and removal at the end of the festival period mirrored the death and resurrection of Jesus.

Today, Carnival is still celebrated all over the world. In the United States, its most famous festival is Mardi Gras in New Orleans, Louisiana, beginning in the weeks leading up to Shrove Tuesday and the start of Lent.

We can also look to the United States for contemporary examples of drawing a metaphorical circle around a space and the rowdy, uninhibited events that take place there. Just consider the motto for Las Vegas, Nevada, a city known for its casinos, shopping, nightlife, and legalized prostitution: "What happens in Vegas, stays in Vegas."

Because these events had an end date in place, it was possible for the Church and Crown to control the ways that people let off steam during these periods of partying.

But in addition to all the drinking and feasting, when people gather in person, interesting things start to happen socially, too. People form bonds with one another and develop a sense of community. They share knowledge with one another. And they discover that there's power in numbers.

As people continued to gather for fairs, services were established to support them, allowing events to grow year to year. Festivals often represented concentrations of economic, political, and religious power, and the rise and fall of many famous festivals reflected the shifting politics of their eras.

Events like Bartholomew Fair in England in 1133 grew to be extraordinarily popular, and the opportunity for trade and commerce was so great that it attracted merchants from the Netherlands, France, and Germany. In the 1600s, it was known for its tournament competitions, acrobats, juggling, and menageries.

Similar events sprang up around Europe. In 1598, Dyrehavsbakken (or Bakken, "the Hill," for short) in Klampenborg, Denmark, attracted visitors because of its natural spring, a welcome alternative to the poor water in Copenhagen at the time. The entertainers followed, of course, until Dyrehavsbakken was deemed off-limits, as it took place on royal hunting grounds.

Between the 1600s and 1800s, events like Bartholomew and Bakken continued to evolve from practical to recreational use, and as they did, so did the entertainments.

But even as these events were controlled and licensed by the clergy, as sentiment and political power shifted, and the general populace began to explore their own power, the festivals were often targeted as sources of moral danger.

In 1618, a man named Robert Dover in the Cotswolds, England, created the "Olimpick Games." King James I directly supported the event, even sending colorful clothes for Dover to wear, in a clear challenge to Puritans' plain dress.

The games ended in 1642 with the outbreak of the English Civil War, a conflict between the Puritans and the supporters of the king. The games were briefly revived, but they shut down again in 1852, when the public grounds were claimed for private ownership.

But you can't keep a good party down for long.

In the 1800s, as canals, steamships, and railroads developed, both Bartholomew and Bakken saw a large growth in popularity and attendance. Bartholomew lasted until it was shut down in 1855 for "vice" and "villainy," but Bakken is still standing today, and is named by the *Guinness Book of World Records* as the "world's oldest amusement park."[6] The Olimpick Games have been run annually since 1963.

Changing economic and travel systems gradually changed the nature of these fairs.

In many cases, trade started concentrating on major, centralized cities. They were easier to reach with ships, and the shift allowed merchants to draw economic control away from the local churches who were taking a cut of the sales.

At the same time, it eliminated the need for regional events to serve as the focal point for economic trade. Happily, the same evolving transportation also allowed the general population to spread out, in search of one thing: fun.

STREETCARS AND TRAINS

Denmark, 1844

A family strolls down a wide brick path, squinting against the sunlight. Everywhere, there is sound: the murmur of conversation, the trickle of music nearby, people laughing from across the field, birds trilling as they hop out of the flower beds, hoping to snatch a bread crumb from people eating lunch.

Suddenly, in the distance, there is the *rat-a-tat-tat* of a drum and the tuning of flutes.

The children perk up. It's time for the parade.

The sound of fifes and drums approaches along with the regular marching of footsteps in sync. A band of children in military dress passes by, their pressed white trousers, bright red jackets, and tall, furry bearskin hats forming unbroken lines of color. They are concentrating hard on their instruments.

This is the Tivoli Youth Guard, a group of children organized to celebrate the second season of Tivoli Gardens, a pleasure garden in Copenhagen. Today, the park is in the heart of the city and spans twenty acres, featuring roller coasters, theaters, carousels, and a Ferris wheel.

While Tivoli Gardens was originally inspired by a different theme park in Paris, it has outlasted most of its competition and is one of the oldest parks today. It is also often cited as the inspiration for Walt Disney creating his own innovative set of parks in the United States.

––––––––––

Where people go, entertainment follows.

During the Gilded Age in the late nineteenth century, industry and commerce thrived. Wealth was unevenly distributed, with industrialists and tycoons at the top of the heap. But as countries around the world shifted from agricultural societies to industrial ones, larger groups of people had more money and fewer working hours.

And with the introduction of the horse-drawn tram in the 1830s, the general populace suddenly had easier, more affordable access to farther-away places.

During this time, streetcar companies used the space at the end of their lines to create trolley parks—picnic and recreation areas that could be used on the weekends—a great way to drum up ridership on an otherwise slow day, since electric companies charged streetcar owners a flat rate whether the trolley was in use or not.

Coney Island in Brooklyn, New York, was one prominent example of an 1820s trolley park that people accessed via horse-drawn streetcar or steamship. By the late 1840s, a ferry line connected to the peninsula's western point, opening it up to the middle classes. The first rail line to connect to Coney Island opened in 1864, and by 1875, expansion of the railway brought one million passengers, which doubled to two million the next year.

In 1843, in Copenhagen, Denmark, Georg Cartensen opened Tivoli Gardens. He had obtained a charter that granted him permission and land by telling King Christian VIII, *"Naar Folket morer sig, laver det ikke Revolution"* ("When the people have fun, they don't make revolution").

When it opened, Tivoli featured bandstands, restaurants, theaters, gardens, and mechanical rides including a roller coaster and a carousel. It was lit by lanterns at night. Today, it remains the second-oldest operating amusement park in the world, and one of the most popular.

The busy era of the mid-1800s also saw the introduction of the first world's fair, Crystal Palace, in London, England, created as a showcase of global industrial achievement.

Technology at that time was rapidly advancing. People were hungry to see it, and many had the time and means to travel for exactly that. Soon after, Paris hosted its own exhibition, and many other cities followed suit.

In many ways, these world's fairs were a cultural turning point, an embodiment of the new freedoms that people experienced as countries—especially the United States—began to shift away from rural centers toward urban ones.

The world's fairs highlighted many types of human innovation and invention, showcasing everything from zippers in 1893 to the X-ray machine in 1901 to the picture phone in 1964. And the world's fairs also saw significant advances in mechanical rides and other types of amusements that would later appear in theme parks, such as the carousel and Ferris wheel.

The Ferris wheel, introduced at the World's Columbian Exposition of 1893 in Chicago, Illinois, was the United States' answer to the Eiffel Tower, created for the 1889 world's fair in Paris. Notable for its use of electric streetlights, the Chicago expo was also the origin of the midway—an area of a carnival or fair set aside for games, amusement rides, food stalls, and entertainment—which is a familiar feature at theme parks to this day.

Trolley parks began to decline in the early 1900s, as cars became the preferred means of transportation.

From the time of the Gilded Age until the Second World War, Coney Island was the largest amusement area in the United States. It set the blueprint for amusement parks as a vacation destination.

CHAPTER 3

The 1950s and 1960s:
Cars and Theme Parks

*I don't want the public to see the world they live in while
they're in the Park. I want them to feel they're in another world.*
—WALT DISNEY

The two world wars changed transportation technology even further. And the postwar boom economy set the stage for the evolution of technology and immersive, interactive entertainment that we enjoy today, including in its current form of escape room games.

Computing technology was created for the world wars, and after the wars ended, that technology continued to develop in laboratories across the world. Every time someone made a new, more advanced computer, someone inevitably made a new, more advanced game to play on it. Alongside the flight simulators and other military uses, scientists were bouncing balls and simulating chess.

At the same time, Americans returned from the war ready to work and ready to spend. Factories converted from producing tanks to manufacturing automobiles. The economy was strong, unemployment was down, and car purchases were high.

People had more spending power, they wanted to be entertained, and they wanted to be able to drive to that entertainment in those shiny new cars.

So, in the 1940s and 1950s, several theme parks opened, including the Disney parks, which exist to this day.

These two branches of entertainment—computers and theme parks—laid the foundation for the Disney empire, now a global enterprise worth billions of dollars that touches the daily lives of people all over the world.

While playing with a brand-new video game console today may seem far removed from riding a roller coaster decorated with cartoon characters or standing in front of a coin-operated game in an arcade, they all share the same DNA, born in war and cultivated in peace.

THE MAGIC KINGDOM

California, United States, 1969
Your eyes are drawn to a huge, run-down manor in the distance, tucked into a stand of trees. You make your way up a winding path, passing a horse-drawn hearse and tombstones sticking out of the ground like teeth.

A wolf howls.

As you get closer, tinkling organ music floats out of the manor's open front doors, drawing you inside. In the parlor, your eyes adjust to the dim lights cast by a cobweb-covered chandelier overhead.

Suddenly, from nowhere and everywhere, a deep voice utters a warning: when strange sounds echo in empty rooms and candles flicker when the air is still, it means that ghosts are present.

An unsmiling butler enters, greeting you and ushering you through a doorway into an odd, octagonal room.

This room is brighter than the foyer. The walls are covered in wood paneling, but along the top of the room are cheerful-looking oil portraits of people. Cheerful, that is, until you notice the creepy gargoyles holding candles that also loom above.

The voice introduces itself as your Ghost Host, welcoming you and your fellow "foolish mortals" to its home.

"Our tour begins here in this gallery," says the Ghost Host. "Where you see paintings of some of our guests as they appeared in their corruptible, mortal state."

Seemingly by magic, the ceiling rises, stretching the walls and revealing more details of the portraits. Where once we saw an elderly woman holding a flower, we now see that she is sitting on top of her husband's grave, shown in the portrait as a stone bust with an ax in its head.

The Ghost Host promises to show you around this haunted house and introduce you to all the spirits within—and you're welcome to join them, if you like.

This is the start of the Haunted Mansion, an attraction that opened at Disneyland in 1969. The "ride" takes place after visitors enter the house, pass through the foyer, and move through the Stretching Room, but the experience of the attraction begins as you approach the building.

The walls that appear to stretch upward are actually a creative solution to a logistical problem: there wasn't enough space to build a full themed attraction, so patrons needed to ride an elevator to another space below, which holds the actual Haunted Mansion ride. The effect became so iconic that the Stretching Room appears in other Disney parks, even though the use of an elevator is no longer necessary.

The problem-solving of the Stretching Room and the thoughtful design of the way patrons experience the Haunted Mansion is an excellent example of Disney's "Imagineering" (from "imagination" and "engineering")—the practical implementation of creative ideas—and the level of quality that can be found in big-budget theme parks.

―――――――

During the late 1800s and early 1900s, popular culture and the nature of cities changed rapidly around the world, shaped by the effects of the Industrial Revolution. People were moving to urban areas, electric street-lights let people stay out longer and later, and motorcars let people travel farther and more easily.

Inspired by the pleasure gardens and amusement parks of the 1800s, the concept of the theme park was perfectly poised to fascinate the postwar, eager American consumer, and it has introduced generations of entertainment seekers to the joys of in-person, experiential entertainment.

After the end of the Second World War, thanks to President Dwight D. Eisenhower's policies and President Franklin D. Roosevelt's New Deal, the economy grew by 37 percent in the 1950s, and unemployment was low, at 4.5 percent. This was also the era of the teenager. The word "teenager" entered common parlance in the 1940s and took on significant cultural meaning in the 1950s, when marketers realized that these youths represented an untapped market of consumers that could be targeted with advertising for specialized goods, clothes, and music.

Having seen the efficient German autobahn during the war, and wanting people to be able to travel quickly in case of a nuclear attack, Eisenhower also funded the development of the US interstate highway system. Factories that had been building tanks and bombs were converted to provide goods for civilians, especially cars.

In 1950, there were twenty-five million automobiles registered in America, most of which had been made before World War II. By 1958, there were more than sixty-seven million.

People had cars, and they wanted to use them.

Trolley parks had been open spaces that anyone could visit using public transportation, and amusement parks charged tickets for each individual ride. But theme parks took things in a new direction. They were the first venues that were enclosed; they charged admission to enter in exchange for access to every ride within, and they featured distinctive design themes.

In 1946, the first theme park in America opened: Santa Claus Land. It was the retirement project of industrialist Louis J. Koch, and featured children's rides, a toy shop, and the year-round opportunity to sit on Santa's lap and ask for presents.

The park was created in Santa Claus, Indiana, a place named in the 1850s by residents who had to pick a new town name when they discovered another Santa Fe in the same state. According to the park's history, Koch, a parent of nine, saw that children visiting the town were disappointed when Santa didn't put in an appearance.

Entrepreneur and animator Walt Disney was similarly inspired by a desire to create a destination for children and families to enjoy.

By the 1940s, Walt Disney Studios was a well-known animation studio, with famous characters like Mickey Mouse, who debuted in the late 1920s, and films like 1937's *Snow White and the Seven Dwarfs*, the first animated feature with full color and sound.

The studio received many visitors, but when they arrived, they found themselves at a workplace, rather than an entertainment destination. Walt Disney was determined to change that.

"Even the people who come to the [Disney] studio," he said, "what do they see? A bunch of guys bending over drawings. Wouldn't it be nice if people could come to Hollywood and see something?"

On August 31, 1948, Disney sent a memo to studio production head Dick Kelsey describing a "Mickey Mouse Park."

He wrote about a central area that would serve as the village green, with a bandstand and benches. Around the green, a village would feature classic small-town attractions like a soda fountain, a toy store, a candy shop, and places to eat. It would be a clean, well-organized space for children and parents to enjoy together, as opposed to carnivals and fairs, which catered to adults and offered alcohol for sale.[1]

Originally, the park was destined for a location near the studio, in Burbank, California, but when the site proved to be too small, the studio purchased a 160-acre plot of land in nearby Anaheim.

Over the next several years, Disney and his team of "Imagineers" studied theme parks and other visitor attractions around the world. In 1951, Disney visited the Tivoli Gardens in Copenhagen, Denmark.

Tivoli originally opened in 1843 on a charter from the Danish king. It had a lovely garden for strolling, bandstands and theaters, restaurants, and mechanical rides similar to roller coasters. It's one of the oldest operating amusements parks to this day.

When Disney visited Tivoli, he already had the concept for a theme park in mind but was charmed by the atmosphere and cleanliness of the Danish amusement park. He took notes on everything he saw: the gardens, the seating, how food was served, the way rides were organized.

Four years later, in 1955, Disney opened Disneyland in California, attracting one million visitors during its first ten weeks.

———————

The main entrance area of Disneyland is themed as Main Street, USA.

To enter this area, visitors must walk under an arch that serves as a visual frame to the tableau beyond. The arch is a bridge for a quaint miniature train that circles the park. A plaque on this arch reads, HERE YOU LEAVE TODAY AND ENTER THE WORLD OF YESTERDAY, TOMORROW AND FANTASY.

From there, visitors look down the main street, with a town square, fictional businesses like dentists and a camera shop, and other locales reminiscent of a small, turn-of-the-century American town. It's a nostalgic "everytown."

Main Street, USA, represents an idealized fantasy version of a small town, like something one might see in a movie, rather than an accurate re-creation of a real-life place. By creating a fantasy, rather than adhering to strict realism, the scene evokes nostalgia with the viewers' understanding that they are in a temporary, liminal, fictional space: the "world of yesterday."

Walking down the main street to the middle of the park, visitors find a large fairy-tale castle. This also serves as a hub that leads to the park's four areas, each featuring a unique theme: Adventureland, Fantasyland, Tomorrowland, and Frontierland.

"Parents can sit in the shade here if they want, while their kids go off into one of the other places," Disney told Bob Thomas in *Walt Disney: An American Original*. "I planned it so each place is right off the hub. You know, when you go to a world's fair, you walk and walk until your feet are sore. I know mine always are. I don't want sore feet here. They make people tired and irritable. I want 'em to leave here happy. They'll be able to cover the whole place and not travel more'n a couple of miles."[2]

The creation of Disneyland marks a major turning point for immersive design, influencing every theme park that came after.

One reason it was so influential is that Disney focused on the experience of the visitor in the parks.

"Don't forget, the biggest attraction isn't here yet," he told Thomas during a tour of the parks.

Thomas asked what he meant.

"People," Disney replied. "You fill this place with people, and you'll really have a show."

Rather than just being a nice garden that people walk through, or a series of decorated buildings, the Disney parks treat their physical areas like stages, and every guest who's welcomed into those areas is a part of the show. (This is also why every employee who works in the Disney parks is called a "cast member.")

Another part of the Disney experience is that when the "show" is on, there are few things to distract people from their sense of immersion in that fantasy world.

There are many examples of how this is put into action in Disney parks, but I want to discuss something totally mundane but very common: garbage.

Garbage in an inevitable part of inviting people into any space. (So are toilets!) So how do you deal with trash in a way that's clean and efficient, doesn't distract people or get in their way, and doesn't break the fantasy of immersion?

As Walt Disney visited carnivals and amusement parks for research, he noticed many problems with garbage. It was such an issue that the design of trash cans in the Disney parks, and how that trash is handled, became an integral part of the experience of visiting Disneyland.

One problem Disney saw was that in many public places, garbage receptacles had no lids. The open-topped bins smelled bad, and when they became full, trash spilled out as people piled more on top. So for his park, Disney developed now-familiar covered bins with swinging lids.

Another issue is that moving garbage around is a big logistics problem. If you've put a garbage can into a busy area, how do you empty it without blocking traffic? How do you move a full bin through a huge crowd? (Not to mention, the process of collecting garbage isn't very magical-looking.)

The bins with swinging lids were one solution for Disneyland. In later parks, like Disney World in Orlando, Florida, the problem of moving garbage was solved with massive, underground pneumatic tubes. These tubes shoot bags of trash toward a central processing area at sixty miles per hour. (There are also long tunnels beneath Disney World so that cast members can move around quickly, and so that costumed characters are never spotted outside of their specific themed area.)

And there's one final story involving Disney and trash that highlights the thought that went into the design of the visitor experience.

It's said that Disney bought a hot dog at a stand in the park and walked down the street, eating it. When he finished the hot dog and looked around for a place to put his used wrapper, he had gone about thirty feet, so a trash can was placed there. Now visitors can eat their hot dogs and throw away their wrappers without even having to think about it—like magic, the garbage can is there, exactly at the moment when it's needed.

This removal of friction is the essence of good experience design and is one of the reasons the Disney parks and the work of the Imagineers who built them are so revered by designers, fans, and millions of visitors alike.

Life is composed of lights and shadows, and we would be untruthful, insincere, and saccharine if we tried to pretend there were no shadows.
—WALT DISNEY

I would be remiss to not mention that Disneyland also popularized the haunted house with the introduction of the Haunted Mansion, a themed "dark ride," or a ride taking place in an illuminated, indoor environment, in 1969.

In the Haunted Mansion, visitors travel through a run-down manor packed with 999 "ghosts," riding a car through a surreal hallway, a séance, a creepy attic, and a graveyard. At the end, they're offered a chance to become the thousandth resident.

Haunted houses share a lot of properties with escape rooms and other immersive works. They move people through a space and must quickly tell stories and convey information through environments and scenes.

Also, Halloween has a lot in common with the medieval festival. It offers a chance for an upending of society, with people able to don fantastical costumes and pretend to be royalty or authority figures for the day. Costume masks give people a chance for anonymous, generally consequence-free revelry. And there is certainly feasting and drinking.

Traditionally, the Halloween holiday used to be more focused on pranks and hooliganism (something medieval people also loved), and like those festivals, the chaos and danger have been largely brought to heel as the holiday has grown both more popular and more commercial.

Now people can get their thrills in a huge range of haunted houses, from do-it-yourself projects in a neighbor's garage, to warehouse-size operations with hundreds of actors and expensive sets and props.

Walt Disney knew that people would be eager for entertainment, and created a venue that brought people together in physical spaces. At the same time, computer technology was rapidly advancing, creating avenues to connect people digitally.

CHAPTER 4

The 1950s–1980s: Computers to Arcades to Consoles

Innovation is hard. It really is. Because most people don't get it.
Remember, the automobile, the airplane, the telephone, these were all
considered toys at their introduction, because they had no constituency.
They were too new.

—NOLAN BUSHNELL, FOUNDER OF ATARI, INC.

To understand the evolution of escape rooms, we first have to dive into the history of computers and how the development of computer technology is connected to game design.

Many advances in technology and transportation originate with the military. Roman roads were laid for the transport of military supplies. World War I is often described as having been started on horses, and finished in tanks.

In 1933, the Third Reich introduced Telex messaging to distribute military messages using modified telephone switches, creating a worldwide communication network.

And by the end of World War II in 1945, room-size computers were breaking military codes and calculating torpedo trajectories. Soon enough, those new technologies would be utilized by civilians. Every time someone created a computer for warfare, someone else invented a way to play with it.

Eventually, those playful experiments became computer games, and as computers evolved away from military use, so did the games themselves.

There have now been five generations of computers, each with more processing power, smaller parts, and faster speeds. As games were developed for these, so, too, were arcade games and at-home entertainment consoles.

THE DAWN OF THE DIGITAL AGE

"Ready or not, computers are coming to the people."

This is how counterculture writer Stewart Brand introduced the first-ever video game into popular discourse in a 1972 *Rolling Stone* article.[1]

In the late sixties and early seventies, computers were still bulky and expensive, limiting them to mostly research facilities and academic use. There were only a few hundred in existence, and a few thousand people able to program them. But a culture was quickly forming around this new technology, and people were paying attention.

The world was undergoing radical change, partially driven by mankind's relationship to computer tech. In 1957, the Sputnik satellites were launched, and in 1969, a man walked on the moon. In the Western world, an antiestablishment cultural movement began to emerge.

There was increasing distrust of the government, fueled by major events like the assassination of US president John F. Kennedy, the civil rights movement, segregation, the changing role of women in the household and the workforce, and a rising awareness of the environmental impact of pollution. There was also major opposition to the war in Vietnam and a push for global nuclear disarmament.

From this stew emerged several subcultures that would shape the development of games, theater, and public gatherings. And as soon as computers were able to display video signals in real time, their programmers were crafting games for them.

LATE NIGHTS IN THE LAB

California, United States, 1972

Laughter and cheers echo down the corridor of the building. Following the noise, you pass fluorescent-lit rooms full of whirring, blinking machines.

Finally, you arrive. A group of young men is clustered around a computer while others surround them, cheering them on.

Looking closer, you can see the setup on a desk: a square screen set into a gray box. A large computer, roughly the size of a refrigerator, whirs nearby.

The young men grasp controllers in their hands, staring intently at the screen as they play a game. Unremarkable by day, this screen is now a portal into a life-or-death tournament of luck and strategy.

On the screen, five rocket ships drift against a starry background. In the middle of the screen, a bright star beckons, the pull of its gravity nearly irresistible. But it must be resisted, or the ships will be destroyed.

The men push on the controllers and the rocket ships fire missiles at one another, bright pixels that litter the playing field as they fly toward their targets.

The ships skid as they zoom around the field, the players anticipating the path of the torpedoes and moving the ships to compensate.

One player pushes their ship too far, though, and it gets sucked into the gravitational pull of the star in the middle of the screen. Half the crowd groans, and the other half applauds.

This is a scene at the Stanford Artificial Intelligence (AI) Laboratory in Palo Alto, California. The students and researchers are playing a version of the first-ever video game, Spacewar, a battle between spaceships. The game uses computing power to calculate trajectory and drag for spaceships and digital torpedoes, displaying them on a monitor.

To contemporary computer users today, this seems simple, maybe even obvious. But at the time, this was revolutionary: the computer that Spacewar ran on, the PDP-1, cost the equivalent of a million dollars today, and only fifty-three existed, mostly in academic, research, and military labs.

In 1964, fourteen people took a road trip from La Honda, California, to New York, riding in a colorful bus. They called themselves the Merry Pranksters, and organized parties with hallucinogens along the way.

Their tie-dyed clothing and antiestablishment philosophies were precursors to the larger hippie movement of the mid-1960s, which centered on San Francisco, a city that would soon become a major hub of today's immersive scene.

One of these Merry Pranksters was Stewart Brand. A part of the Haight-Ashbury scene in San Francisco, Brand had his finger on the pulse of popular culture, as an observer, instigator, and reporter.

For example, in 1966, he campaigned for NASA to release a satellite image of the entire earth, something which had never been seen before. He believed that seeing the planet as one unified system would be a powerful and inspirational symbol, and a call to people to care for our shared home.

That image would later become the first cover of Brand's counterculture project, the *Whole Earth Catalog*, a directory of tools and information to help the reader "find his own inspiration, shape his own environment, and share his adventure with whoever is interested."[2]

In December 1968, engineer Douglas Engelbart gave a demonstration at a computer conference in San Francisco. The session was titled "A Research Center for Augmenting Human Intellect." Brand assisted, running the cameras and helping the production run smoothly.

During the session, Engelbart moved a computer mouse around a screen, making and changing lists of text and moving and resizing windows.

Using the computer, he video-conferenced with his laboratory in Menlo Park, California, chatting with a person on the other end as they collaboratively edited a document. He even clicked on a link to open up a new page.

Watching the recording online today, all these actions seem perfectly ordinary. But back then, the audience had never seen anything like it. They gave him a standing ovation. Today, this presentation is known colloquially as "The Mother of All Demos."

Remember—this was 1968. The year of Vietnam War protests and the assassination of Martin Luther King Jr. In 1968, the Boeing 747 jumbo jet flew for the first time, and Apollo 8 orbited the moon—where Apollo 11 would land the following year.

And while several of these concepts were being explored in other labs and research facilities, this presentation introduced them to the industry of imagination.

Today, we can easily see its influence and how it pushed the conceptualization of these ideas forward, although it would be years before these tools were utilized in computers and Internet development.

Brand recognized the potential impact that computers would have on humanity. Several years after "The Mother of All Demos," he was writing an article for *Rolling Stone* about the campus subculture that had sprung up around computer programming.

"Ready or not, computers are coming to the people," he wrote as the opening salvo. "How mass use of computers might go is not even slightly known as yet, except for obvious applications in the schools. One informative place to inquire is among the hackers, particularly at night when they're pursuing their own interests."[3]

He toured around laboratories and saw not just the raw computing power of the machines but also the potential for humans to connect with them and use them for transformation of the self and the culture around us.

Brand described the programmers he met as "the technicians of this science . . . They are the ones who translate human demands into code that the machines can understand and act on. . . . Those magnificent men with their flying machines, scouting a leading edge of technology which has an odd softness to it; outlaw country, where rules are not decree or routine so much as the starker demands of what's possible."

It's a romantic description, and in 2018, Brand clarified his position, stating that "most of the real engineering was done by people with narrow ties who worked nine to five, often with federal money."[4]

But in 1972, he wrote about a man using the lab computers to calculate the complicated household finances of his commune, and talked about people creating programs that would automatically generate protest letters, addressed to your congressmen, if they typed in their name and address.

He was especially drawn to the performance and competition of video games.

"There were always some young engineers gathered around the

computer blasting away at this game Spacewar," Brand said in a retro-spective *Rolling Stone* interview in 2016.[5]

We would now call this genre of entertainment "e-sports," recogniz-ing that there's an appeal to observing the spectacle of a team sport, whether it's digital or in person. Brand wanted to describe this excite-ment to his readers, so he organized a Spacewar tournament at Stan-ford, offering a case of beer as a prize. It was the first e-sports reporting ever.

Spacewar started as a collaborative, open-source[*] project.

In 1962, young programmer Steve Russell was with the electrical engineering department at the Massachusetts Institute of Technology (MIT).

The school had a PDP-1, a "minicomputer" about the height of one refrigerator and the depth of three refrigerators. It came with a console typewriter, a paper-tape reader, and a separate CRT monitor, a round screen set into a trapezoidal-shaped box.

Russell and his friends wanted to create interesting visual displays that would show off the capabilities of the computer. They were fans of science fiction books, especially a series with lots of ship fights in space. So when it came time to design a game, they drew from the scenes of dogfights in space.

One of the important things in Spacewar is the pace. It's relatively fast-paced, and that makes it an interesting game. It seems to be a reasonable compromise between action—pushing buttons—and thought. Thought does help you, and there are some tactical consider-ations, but just plain fast reflexes also help.

---

[*]Open-source software contains code that is shared publicly for other programmers to access, study, and develop further.

It was quite interesting to fiddle with the parameters, which of course I had to do to get it to be a really good game. By changing the parameters you could change it anywhere from essentially just random, where it was pure luck, to something where skill and experience counted above everything else. The normal choice is somewhere between those two. With Spacewar an experienced player can beat an amateur for maybe 20 to 50 games and then the amateur begins to win a little.[6]

"The game of Spacewar blossoms spontaneously wherever there is a graphics display connected to a computer," said Alan Kay in the 1972 *Rolling Stone* article.

When games are being played, it's natural for people to gather around them to see the spectacle. With the advent of the transistor and microchip, gameplay tech suddenly became far more accessible to the public.

This leap forward in technology sowed the seeds of contemporary video games, and those seeds were planted in physical spaces, first in public with the arcade, and then in private with the video game console.

A NEW WAVE

Sunnyvale, California, August 1972
Cigarette smoke hangs heavy in the air. A strange pinging and buzzing can be heard over the din of the bar patrons talking and laughing, drifting out of an anteroom of the bar.

Heading in, we see two people standing in front of a tall, narrow wooden box, next to a pinball table.

The box has instructions:

DEPOSIT QUARTER

BALL WILL SERVE AUTOMATICALLY

AVOID MISSING BALL FOR HIGH SCORE

The people are shoulder to shoulder, nudging one another to get a better look at a black-and-white television screen embedded in the box, and their faces glow in the pale light.

On the screen, a small white ball bounces between paddles, like a tennis ball moving across the court. Leaning toward the box, each person has their hand on a dial, which they spin back and forth, moving a digital paddle up or down to receive the ball and return it to their opponent's side of the court.

The ball misses a paddle, and the game ends. Someone fishes in their pocket for another quarter and drops it in the machine.

There's a line of people behind them, waiting their turn.

This is Pong, the first arcade game.

According to legend, it was extremely popular when it was first installed, but it began to experience some sort of technical problem. When the technicians were called in, they found the source of the problem: the coin box was so full it was overflowing, and somehow it interfered with the machine.

Whether this anecdote is true or not, Pong, and the company that created it, Atari, would have a major influence on public and private play spaces.

As computers got smaller and games got more fun, their shift from laboratories to the arcade was inevitable.

Pinball machines with electronic components had been popular in amusement parks and midways since their introduction in the 1930s. As the machines evolved in the forties and fifties to include moving parts like flippers, they changed from games of chance to games of skill, a distinction that drew a line between "gambling" and "amusement."

The early video game Spacewar spread around the programming community in the sixties and seventies, inspiring the first-ever arcade cabinets—tall wooden boxes that housed the screens and hardware—which kicked off a golden age of arcade games.

Young engineer Nolan Bushnell played Spacewar while attending MIT in the sixties, and in 1971, working with Ted Dabney, he created the first arcade video game, Computer Space.

The screen for Computer Space was housed in a cool fiberglass cabinet with smooth curves. It was so futuristic-looking that in 1973, a Computer Space cabinet appeared in the film *Soylent Green* as an example of the sort of advanced entertainment technology we might find in the year 2022.

The Computer Space cabinet was considered somewhat successful. It was a commercial success, making over a million dollars in sales, but it failed to catch fire in the way its manufacturers had hoped.

Bushnell parted ways with the manufacturer and used the money to found Atari, which would introduce the world to the concept of video games.

In 1972, Bushnell asked employee Allan Alcorn to create a simple two-player table tennis game: Pong.

The gameplay is simple but strong. It is a digital version of table tennis: two vertical lines representing paddles slide up and down the left and right sides of the screen, each controlled by a player. They volley a small dot between them, trying to catch it as it changes angles or speeds up.

Alcorn created a prototype with a black-and-white television in a wooden cabinet, which they installed in Andy Capp's Tavern, a local bar.

It turned out to be extremely popular, and the company pivoted to manufacture more arcade machines. (Bushnell attributed the game's success to the fact that it required two players, allowing a person to approach others at a bar to see if they'd like a game. Carrying this lesson about the power of in-person play forward, he later founded the family-friendly Chuck E. Cheese pizza and games restaurant chain.)

In 1975, Atari released a home version of Pong, which was a success both commercially—selling 150,000 units—and culturally, with the media recognizing the home video game console as the start of a new generation of entertainment and design.

The rules and procedures that guide the player as they interact with a game are called "mechanics." These mechanics dictate how the game reacts to the actions of the player.

A game mechanic can be anything from a rule requiring players to roll dice before moving spaces in a board game, to the way that players are able to rotate and drop shapes in Tetris. Together, these actions and reactions make up what we call gameplay.

In 1977, the Atari 2600 was released, introducing two types of puzzle games: some were based on previously existing mechanics, including a digital version of the Rubik's Cube; others were totally new designs.

The ability to create puzzle games digitally led to the creation of many new mechanics that hadn't been seen before. In 1982, Hiroyuki Imabayashi released Sokoban for the PC-8801. Sokoban is played on a game board divided into squares, with some "wall" squares and some "passage" squares. Its mechanic is pushing crates through the passages around a warehouse, and its gameplay is pushing these crates onto goals while avoiding trapping them in corners against walls.

But it was in 1989 that digital puzzle games really took off, all thanks to Tetris.

Tetris was created in 1984 by Alexey Pajitnov. In Tetris, players are presented with a vertical screen. At the top of the screen, blocks in various shapes appear. These fall toward the bottom and can be rotated by the player. As they touch the bottom, they begin to pile up, forming rows of blocks. If a row of blocks is completely filled by the shapes, it will disappear, making more room for blocks to fall.

As the software made its way across the world, the game became popular both on home computers and in arcades. In 1989, Tetris was bundled with the release of the handheld Nintendo Game Boy console.

In a 2014 interview with the *Guardian*, Dutch video game publisher Henk Rogers described brokering the deal with Nintendo: "Tetris made Game Boy and Game Boy made Tetris. It was the perfect platform for the game, since you could carry it around. That's how it caught on."[7]

In addition to puzzle games, the late eighties and nineties saw a boom of text-based adventures. These games were often based on navigating through classic setups, like carefully making your way through a fantasy-world dungeon to find a magical golden key.

But gameplay also took a turn toward the tangible during this era. People were still playing adventure games, but they were crafting these games for themselves and acting out all the parts. And written game systems like Dungeons & Dragons gave them a vocabulary with which to do it.

CHAPTER 5

The 1970s and 1980s: Dungeons & Dragons and Larp

You are not entering this world in the usual manner, for you are setting forth to be a Dungeon Master. . . . [A]s DM you are to become the Shaper of the Cosmos. It is you who will give form and content to all the universe. You will breathe life into the stillness, giving meaning and purpose to all the actions which are to follow.

—GARY GYGAX, COCREATOR OF DUNGEONS & DRAGONS

Play in the 1970s and '80s was blossoming everywhere: on computers, in shared public spaces like arcades, and at home. There was a thriving community of people using the power of their imaginations to render rich creative scenes for themselves and their friends.

Dungeons & Dragons, arguably the most famous role-playing game in the world, originated in the 1970s.

Around the same time, live-action role play, or larping, gained popularity alongside a resurgence in hobbyist historical re-creation.

These communities developed their own vocabularies of play and introduced people to systematic improvisation. In addition to creative, collaborative storytelling, character-making, and world-building, there are also ample opportunities for artistic expression through makeup and costuming, careful painting of detailed miniature figurines, making art of characters and events, handmaking resin dice, and the crafting of gaming accessories.

As always, these are just newer manifestations of types of play that humans have been engaging in throughout recorded memory, beginning with the war games of the ancient Romans, to Tudor pageants that were emulated hundreds of years later by the Victorians, to hobbyists reenacting historical battles and medievalists attending Renaissance fairs.

AT THE TABLE

A group of teens sits around a table. At the head of the table, a boy looks at the papers spread out in front of him, a small folding screen obscuring the other kids' views. He has hand-drawn maps, stacks of notes, and a slim printed book.

He is the dungeon master, leading his friends through a play session of Dungeons & Dragons, a fantasy tabletop role-playing game.

The dungeon master describes a scene: Their characters are standing outside a tavern in a new town, where they are strangers. Their goal is to get information from a ranger who's inside the tavern.

The players confer with one another. One suggests, only half joking, that they should kick down the door, holding up the tavern like a bank heist and demanding the info.

The others point out that none of them have particularly strong weapons, and may in fact be defeated by the door before they even get inside.

Eventually, it's agreed that the group will try flattery first, then bribery, to get the information they need.

The players enter the tavern and speak to the barkeeper. The dungeon master acts out the lines, informing them that the ranger is in an upstairs room.

"Okay, *now* we kick down the door," the overeager player says.

The teammates shrug. After all, the inner doors are probably weaker up there, so why not?

The dungeon master's hand hovers over a set of many-sided plastic dice.

"Are you sure you want to do that?" he asks, making eye contact with one of the players.

They don't take the hint and proceed to kick down the door of the tavern, entering it without looking inside first. They are quickly consumed by a gelatinous cube.

This is Dungeons & Dragons. Once scorned by wider culture, it's now (correctly) recognized as a popular imaginative pastime that encourages collaboration and is enjoying a resurgence among young gamers. In the late 2010s, sales grew by 30 percent for five years in a row, and there are many celebrity fans, including actors Joe Manganiello, Vin Diesel, and Deborah Ann Woll.

The story of Dungeons & Dragons began in 1971 when Gary Gygax and Jeff Perren wrote a war game to simulate medieval combat, Chainmail.

War games are battle enactments played with miniature figures on a large, often very detailed tabletop battlefield. The figures represent military models of soldiers, vehicles, and weaponry.

The gameplay is usually turn-based, as each player moves their figurines across the battlefield to mount attacks. The outcomes of these battles are calculated with math and can be influenced by dice rolls.

This style of gameplay originated in Prussia in 1780, created by Johann

Christian Ludwig Hellwig to teach military strategy to army officers in training, and as a commercial game for the general public.

Hellwig's game, inspired by chess, played out on a grid of color-coded squares representing different types of terrain, with players moving figures once per turn to try to capture or destroy enemy pieces.

It was very commercially successful. Later imitators introduced new mechanics, including dice rolls to introduce the element of chance.

War games were adopted by the Prussian army in 1824 for training and research and slowly grew popular with the public over the next hundred years.

In 1913, author H. G. Wells published *Little Wars*, considered the first rule book for miniature war gaming. Although he introduced new innovations to the genre, like a three-dimensional battlefield, there was a metal shortage due to the war that hindered the creation of soldier figures.

War gaming picked up again after the real-life war ended, with the creation of figurines and publication of books and manuals in the United States and England.

Until the mid 1950s, war games generally dealt with real-life armies and scenarios. In 1956, Tony Bath created a set of rules for use in war games set in ancient times. This rule set inspired Gygax's Chainmail in 1971, which provided rules to be used in a fantasy setting and introduced characters like wizards and elves.

In the seventies, interest in epic fantasy worlds was rising. While J. R. R. Tolkien's *The Lord of the Rings: The Fellowship of the Ring* was published in 1954, it didn't gain critical cultural mass until the 1960s, when it was reprinted in a cheap, soft-cover book form.

Gygax collaborated with a friend, Dave Arneson, to develop what they then termed the Fantasy Game, a mix of the characters and world of J. R. R. Tolkien's Lord of the Rings and Robert E. Howard's Conan the Barbarian.

They created a pencil-and-paper role-playing game, designed for players sitting at the same table. An additional player, the dungeon master, or DM, runs the game, keeping the story flowing, acting as non-player characters (NPCs), and refereeing the actions of the players as they move through the fictional world.

One feature of this style of game is that each player creates a unique character, marking down their statistics and abilities, which will affect the actions they can make during gameplay.

Parallel to the development of Dungeons & Dragons, with its in-person play and rich worlds of imagination and customized characters, another form of gameplay was emerging: live-action role play.

Live-action role play, or larp, is exactly what it sounds like. Players take on character roles, act out scenes, and tell stories in person. Games can have many themes, from sci-fi to vampires to historical reenactment.

People have been larping since ancient times, staging mock battles and putting on pageants and performances that today we would categorize as being "immersive." In her book *Leaving Mundania*, Lizzie Stark describes a pageant put on for Queen Elizabeth I of England:

> Such Tudor pageants are similar to larp in terms of structure and presentation. The action isn't presented for an audience locked behind the fourth wall; it's dispersed, presented dynamically, with costumed actors appearing in the woods, on a pond, behind castle walls, and so on. The queen is in the midst of the action, and she is involved in the outcomes of the various plots.[1]

As with many games, there's no single origin for larping, as people have enjoyed costumed role play throughout history.

In the United States, military reenactments, or "sham battles," have a long and popular tradition. To this day, during festivals, citizens often dress as Revolutionary War figures, and holidays feature "shams"—partly for entertainment, partly to acclimate regular citizens to the idea of seeing themselves as soldiers.

Immediately following the Civil War, people role-played battles from it. On the fiftieth anniversary of the Battle of Gettysburg, fifty thousand veterans gathered in reunion, and the festivities included reenactments of the battle.

In the 1960s, one hundred years after the Civil War, these re-creations reappeared, with a staging of the First Battle of Bull Run taking place in July 1961.

As Dungeons & Dragons became more popular in the 1970s and epic fantasy fiction rose in culture, fantasy larps also found their place, as people desired to take the action off the table and into the real world.

Throughout the eighties, larps spread around the world, springing up in England, Russia, New Zealand, as well as Sweden, Finland, and Norway, and in the nineties, rule books were published by official publishers.

One also can't discuss larp without talking about the Nordic style that emerged as a movement in the late nineties.

Nordic larp is more avant-garde than other types of larping, with unobtrusive rules and a desire to explore and expose beliefs. Their stories tend to focus on topics that are more intense, personal, or political, and often gameplay is collaborative rather than combat-based, allowing for deep self-expression and an atmosphere of immersion.

There is an awareness of the temporary communities created by these experiences, and that games "are a natural tool for studying questions such as what kind of a world is possible, what the world should or could be like—and what our world is actually like."[2]

Between at-home tabletop games and video game consoles, the public at large was starting to have a greater exposure to games and their story-telling possibilities. They were beginning to get a taste for adventure. And when the nineties hit, a whole new generation of the populace would get that game vocabulary for themselves through the medium of television.

CHAPTER 6

The 1970s–1990s: A Game Vocabulary for the Public

To get a game show into production is as challenging and as intellectually demanding as it is to write a novel or screenplay. Getting Millionaire *right was as hard as writing* Dirty Pretty Things. *Harder. In the pilots, contestants kept wanting to take the money; we had to find ways—the lifelines—of keeping them in the seat, answering the questions. But there is so much snobbery about popular culture. A game show just isn't valued as much as a novel.*
—STEVEN KNIGHT, COCREATOR OF *WHO WANTS TO BE A MILLIONAIRE*

Quiz shows have long dominated popular gaming culture, from radio programs in the 1930s to television right up to the present day. Many stalwarts have been around for ages—*Jeopardy!*, *The Price Is Right*, *Family Feud*, and *Wheel of Fortune*.

In the 1990s, just before the dawn of the Internet age, we began to see new innovations in quiz shows that would lay the groundwork for today's game-friendly, puzzle-inclined culture. These shows gave people a working vocabulary for gameplay, team building, and tackling challenges, just as the advent of home computers made games more accessible and CD-ROM puzzle games wowed the world.

TUNE IN

A team of six people races along an industrial walkway, grabbing the handrails for balance.

Each of them wears a different-colored full-body jumpsuit: yellow, green, blue, red, maroon, and silver.

They're following a spry bald man in a leopard-patterned frock coat who leaps about, commentating in a pirate voice and apologizing for the water streaming from above.

This group is on board the SS *Atlantis*, and their host has commanded them to gain entry into to Ocean Zone, where their game will begin.

The group unhitches a rope from a wall, revealing a narrow portal. They clamor down a rope net and race along metal grates, avoiding the splashing droplets.

Finally, they emerge into a ship's ornate grand salon, in the style of the *Titanic*, with columns and statues.

"Let's play a game," the host says, leading the group to a door in the ship's interior. The door opens, a player climbs inside, and the clock begins.

These people are on a game show called *The Crystal Maze*, and the gamboling host is Richard O'Brien, creator of *The Rocky Horror Picture Show*.

The Crystal Maze was a game show that first ran for several years in the United Kingdom, starting in 1990. It was based on a French game show, *Fort Boyard*, in which people race around an 1800s fortress, tackling mini-challenges and solving riddles.

On *The Crystal Maze,* players moved around a fantasy set, entering small chambers that contained a variety of gamelike challenges and puzzles, and gaining round "crystals" for each successfully completed room. Each crystal could be redeemed later in the game for more time to earn prize money.

Some of the challenges were distinctly escape room–like, with a series of linear puzzles that had to be solved so that the game could continue.

It was an unconventional show, but it struck the right note with the audience, earning it a devoted following and inspiring many future game designers.

———————

Game shows on the radio and television have gone through many evolutions. The first popular radio quiz shows aired in the late 1930s, and the first television quiz shows began in 1941.

In the 1950s, daytime television featured many quiz shows that established a now-familiar template: people compete to win large cash prizes, often returning to the next day's show if they win. Like the radio programs that preceded them, these shows were built around contestants answering general-knowledge questions.

Several quiz shows, including *The $64,000 Question, Dotto,* and *Twenty-One,* were rigged by the producers to control the narrative of the show. By feeding contestants answers in advance, they were able to keep entertaining guests on and hook viewers into story lines about the contestants' challenges and triumphs. The contestants became stars.

So when some contestants were asked to lose in order to allow a new star to take their place, or were set up to lose by the production, they were, unsurprisingly, pretty unhappy. After one contestant sued her show for setting her up to lose, and another contestant leaked the fact that he had been fed answers in advance, the Federal Trade Commission (FTC) opened an investigation. When the accusations turned out to be true, Congress made rigging quiz shows illegal, and the shows were all canceled.

(There's a fun movie about this, *Quiz Show*, from 1994, if you want a peek into this era of television.)

It took a long time for television programs to recover after the quiz show scandal. In the 1960s, networks introduced new quiz shows with lower stakes, like *Jeopardy!* (1964) and panel shows featuring celebrities answering trivia and cracking jokes.

By the late sixties, a counterculture revolution was taking place, and viewers were less receptive to television shows set in idyllic small towns with no connection to the problems and stories of the age. Many rural-focused shows like *The Andy Griffith Show* and *The Beverly Hillbillies* were replaced with stories about working-class families (*All in the Family* and its spin-offs *Maude* and *The Jeffersons*), single women making their way in the workplace (*The Mary Tyler Moore Show*), and people serving in the Korean War (*M*A*S*H*).

But it wasn't until the 1970s that major attention and money were devoted to this type of mass-appeal TV show—"Quiz shows," which had been perceived as "highbrow" programs dealing with knowledge questions and featuring highly educated, intelligent contestants, became "game shows" to attract a broader, everyman audience.

During this time, *The Price Is Right, Family Feud*, and *Wheel of Fortune* debuted, all of which have continued to air for nearly half a century, but other shows didn't fare nearly as well, and throughout the eighties and early nineties, they were mostly phased out.

This is where things start to get really interesting for game designers and puzzle lovers, though.

In the early nineties, several shows focusing on puzzles, intrigue, strategy, and gameplay debuted that would prove to be deeply influential to the immersive scene that would follow in later decades.

In 1990, *The Crystal Maze* debuted on Channel 4 in the United Kingdom.

It took place on the biggest set in the country and was hosted by Richard O'Brien. It was originally going to be an English-language version of a French program called *Fort Boyard*. But the fort was under construction and not available for filming, so they decided to create their own format.

"The original set looked more like a light entertainment set, a bit like a traditional game show," said James Dillon in an interview with *BuzzFeed*.[1] "But that was a mistake, to think this was a game show rather than some sort of exciting world you could enter into and have an adventure in. Once we'd got away from the concept of it being a studio-based game to it being a traveling adventure, it became clearer what we'd have to do."

On *The Crystal Maze*, teams of players passed through elaborately decorated sets, themed as "Industrial," "Ocean," "Aztec," and "Futuristic" zones.

Within each zone were many doors—originally six per zone—each containing a challenge or puzzle in a twelve-by-twelve-foot room.

There were four types of challenges waiting behind the doors: physical, mental, skill, and "mystery," and over the course of an episode, players tackled twelve or thirteen different rooms.

Each challenge took two to three minutes to play. The player's goal was to solve the challenges and obtain a small round crystal while their teammates observed through a little window and cheered them on, or shouted as they tried to direct the player's attention to missed details or solutions in the room.

If the player successfully completed the challenge, they could grab the crystal and dash back to the door. If they ran out of time, they were locked in, and their team could choose whether to spend a crystal to free them, or leave them behind for the rest of the game. (Ouch.)

The earned crystals could be redeemed for time in the game's finale, the Crystal Dome, which had people standing in a huge, multifaceted orb, snatching flying metallic paper out of the air.

One of the most magical things about *The Crystal Maze* was the energy given to it by Richard O'Brien. He had been encouraged to "be himself" as the host character, choosing his own over-the-top wardrobe and doing commentary in his own words rather than using a script designed for a character.

The production stumbled upon a trope that helped differentiate the show and fuel its success: O'Brien speaking directly to the audience during gameplay.

"I just started talking into the camera, about anything," O'Brien told *BuzzFeed*. "I was just trying to make the cameraman laugh, and as soon as I saw the camera shaking on his shoulders I'd look back at the clock and say, 'Okay, half a minute to go.'"

The production team didn't even realize they had any of these asides until they started editing, and once they did, they realized how that worked—"a quick cutaway of me saying, 'They'll never manage this,' or I'd pull out the harmonica, and unknowingly it added a complicity between me and the audience at home because I was looking straight into the camera. I never did it when the contestants were there, only when their backs were turned."

It was a lot of fun, thanks to the personality of the host, the team dynamics, and the exciting design of the sets. For the viewer, in many ways, it's akin to watching a sport: you cheer for some people and boo others, argue with your friends, get wrapped up in the adventure.

The format of the game had many parallels to immersive design, with themed sets, underlying lore, and a variety of tasks to complete.

And occasionally, the mystery challenge was what we would now consider an escape room: a linear series of puzzles that led eventually to a final solution, opening the locked door for the competitor to escape and return to the rest of their team. Even the clues weren't too far from what you might find in an actual escape room today.

The Crystal Maze ended in 1995, and was Channel 4's top-rated show the entire time it was on the air, with millions of viewers.

By the end of its original tenure, after eighty-three episodes, only six teams had ever reached a perfect score of ten crystals.

But it fed the imagination of an entire generation of kids who longed to have adventures in those themed sets. (For a time in the nineties, they could, by visiting a Cyberdrome Crystal Maze, interactive games with replica sets, with locations in the UK, Japan, and Dubai.)

It demonstrated to the public that these sorts of puzzle games could be fun challenges undertaken as a team. People could see themselves in those roles (if not the silly jumpsuits), and more important, they now had a way to talk about the design and format of these games.

Throughout the nineties and into the 2000s, producers realized that a combination of reality and game show—for example, *Survivor*, *The Mole*, and *Real World/Road Rules Challenge*—was a winning formula. By combining personal narratives with gameplay and strategy, they could draw in viewers and create a culture around the show, just as the original quiz shows had done. Plus, the everyday viewer could discuss games and gameplay with the vocabulary they had learned from television, and internalize new rules and structures for how play could progress, look, and feel.

The stage was set for the escape room era.

PLUG IN

The world is dark. You open your eyes.

You find yourself standing on a dock, the sound of waves hitting the shore loud in your ears.

In the water to your right, a ship is fully submerged, with only the tops of its masts emerging from the glassy, green surface.

Ahead of you, stairs lead up to what appear to be giant gears embedded in a rocky hillside. To your left, more stairs lead to a group of buildings on a hill scattered with trees and pillars.

What are you supposed to do? No instructions present themselves, and there are no people nearby to explain anything to you. All you can do is look around, and move forward.

You tentatively make your way up some stairs and notice your first clue. It's a note, written in elegant script on crumpled paper:

> *Catherine,*
>
> *I've left for you a message of utmost importance in our fore-chamber beside the dock. Enter the number of Marker Switches on this island into the imager to retrieve the message.*
>
> *Yours,*
> *Atrus*

You explore the island, climbing stairs and going inside intriguing buildings. All around you are strange levers and buttons. Pushing one, you hear a clanking noise on the other side of the island, a sure sign that a new puzzle or mystery has been revealed.

This is Myst, an adventure game released in 1993 by Cyan, Inc. It was a surprise bestseller, charming millions of people with its unusual story-telling and nonviolent approach.

It has remained one of the most popular games of all time and is credited with popularizing the CD-ROM for home computer use. It inspired many puzzle games and is frequently cited as an inspiration for immersive work.

CD-ROMs

By the late eighties, home computers were becoming more common, increasingly purchased by average users rather than hobbyists. Computer marketing had largely tried to avoid associating the machines with games, desiring a broader range of home users.

It may also have been partly due to the video game crash of 1983, or "Atari shock," a video-game recession caused by oversaturation in the console market, with fifteen million consoles sold and overproduction of game cartridges.

"Too many machines are chasing too few quarters," said a president of a vending machine corporation in a 1983 *New York Times* article, which also predicted a "pronounced movement from game machines to home computers, which can figure a family's budget as well as transport the player to outer space."[2]

The crash also led to the closure of fifteen hundred arcades out of an estimated ten thousand in the United States.

But by 1986, video game consoles like the Nintendo Entertainment System (NES) dominated stores, and home consoles rose again.

Both home computing and video game consoles had been dismissed as fads, but it seems that people weren't willing to let them go quite so easily.

By the 1990s, both video game consoles and home computers were commonplace, and the hunger for games was greater than ever.

———————

The game Myst launched for Mac in September 1993, and for IBM PC in February 1994, and it seriously shook things up.

"A new art form may arise from the 'Myst,'" declared a *New York Times* headline (although it also declared that the milestone of a new art form was "still a ways off. . . . Its reflective, almost cool esthetic, though, gives a hint of what may eventually be possible, as the technology improves: a game that weaves together image, sound and narrative into a new form of experience"[3]).

Myst is about a mysterious book that has fallen into a rift. On its pages are windows into intriguing lands, and when a player clicks the image, they're transported there, a lone traveler dropped into a strange world.

The game is in the first person, and players interact with the environment, locating switches, levers, wheels, and buttons around a set of mysterious islands with Jules Verne–like contraptions and buildings. Some of the switches and levers cause parts of the island to react, while others function as combination locks.

The design of the islands in the game is strange and mysterious. There is a real eeriness to the world, even though there are no threats present, no enemies to kill or characters to talk to. But the emptiness of the islands is intriguing, rather than frightening. As the player, you're known only as "the Stranger."

It has none of the things that were features of most console and arcade games at the time: no guns, no inventory, no death, no enemies popping out to kill you, no score, no time limit, no weapons, no tools.

Also, there are no obvious instructions. The only options are to explore the beautiful landscapes and intriguing buildings, and solve the mechanical puzzles you find there. You don't have to be particularly skilled at using the computer, either; all you have to do is click.

"I think it was just that we intuitively didn't like the artifice of game stuff, and we didn't see a reason for it," Myst cocreators Robyn and Rand Miller told *Grantland*'s Emily Yoshida in 2013.[4] "We just felt like there was no reason for buttons, and if you're playing a game, you should be in that world as much as possible. It's a story and a world, and when you go to the movies, you don't have to deal with that kind of thing."

The game is built on a system called HyperCard, a series of linked cards that function almost like presentation software you might use in an office setting. The visuals in Myst were pre-rendered, with occasional animations and video clips. (A minor spoiler: you do eventually meet characters in the game, who teach you more about the world of Myst.)

Upon release, it was extremely popular, and it introduced people to a new way of thinking about games: they didn't have to be competitive or violent, but could actually be introspective and beautiful.

It's worth noting that several other big games were released in 1993, including puzzle video games like Trilobyte Games' The 7th Guest and LucasArts' Day of the Tentacle.

Another major 1993 release, Doom, was violent and did have weapons and tons of action. Doom was a fast-paced first-person shooter (FPS) game, which was also radically new. Like Myst, it changed how people thought about the potential of games.

And between these titles, a lot more people bought computers that could play CD-ROMs.

Myst had an impact on its audience, certainly—by 2000 it had sold more than 6.3 million copies worldwide, and was the top-selling PC game in the United States until 2002, nearly nine years after its initial release.

Today, it's frequently cited as a source of inspiration for immersive work, puzzle games, and story-driven experiences.

But twenty years after its release, in 2013, its impact on the games industry was less clear.

In the *Grantland* interview, Rand Miller said that interest in this type of exploratory, puzzle-heavy, narrative "adventure game" "just kind of puttered out."

It was as if the game was almost too good. "It was kind of weird: We got accolades for increasing the exposure of what was called the 'adventure game' and then we got blamed on the other hand for the death of the adventure game, because it was too big and too hard to top it," Miller said.

Today, there are many successful, independently produced games set in beautiful environments and telling interesting narratives with puzzles, and they all owe a debt to Myst for paving the way.

It's perhaps no surprise, though, that CD-ROM-based story and puzzle games had a high point that faded away. It would be hard for any game to outshine the piece of tech that came along next: the Internet.

But before the Internet arrived to change the world as we know it, people were exploring new, creative ways of using space and gathering in person.

CHAPTER 7

The 1980s–2020s: New Ways of Looking at Shared Spaces

The difference between immersive experience and traditional experience
is the presence of a viewing port, proscenium, or a frame
with which to take in the experience.
—SARA THACHER, IMAGINEER

Let's stop for a moment and talk about "immersive."

"Immersive work" is an umbrella term for everything we've discussed so far. It can be theater or virtual reality, an audio experience, a game that plays out across the Internet and in real life, or a private ritual done by oneself.

No Proscenium, an online publication covering the immersive entertainment space, defines immersion as "an experience that physically and (usually) narratively puts the audience in the same place in which the action occurs."

Theaters are built with a frame around the stage, known as the proscenium arch. Immersive work has no frame, whether that's the computer screen, the television, or the theater stage.

Immersive art is something that you experience without borders.

At the same time that computers were being built, games were evolving and the Internet was being created, there were also several hotbeds of experiential design that have turned out to be very influential in immersive work.

Let's talk about San Francisco and London. (Other cities like Seattle and Boston have their own histories as puzzle-friendly cities and have since risen as focal points for escape rooms, but we'll discuss those later, and many global cities have their own long legacies.)

San Francisco is a city founded on a gold rush, and it has long been a home to people looking to make their way in the world, become lost, or find themselves. (Sometimes all three at once.)

In London, rave culture and festivals have led to an audience receptive to immersive work that decenters the art object as something you move around to look at.

Many cultural movements have passed through these cities, all weaving a larger tapestry of immersive work, radical usage of sites and installations, and collaboration and teamwork.

SAN FRANCISCO AND BLACK ROCK CITY

A giant bonfire crackles. You're far away but can still feel the heat radiating off it. Fireworks pop in the sky above, and the land spreads out flat all around you.

Everything around seems to be adorned with glowing lights: neon bike tires, bobbing candlelit lanterns, ribbons of light running up a massive sculpture overhead, the clothes of a group of people walking nearby.

Revelers are silhouetted against the night sky. A man dances wearing neon stripes head to toe.

You pass through a tunnel of lights as colorful bikers cycle by, playing music, the notes fading in the night air, mixing with the laughter and chatter of thousands of other people.

You wander through a maze of tall tents. Craning your neck to look upward, you see a projected kaleidoscope of light and patterns.

People climb up a tower of cars stacked several stories high, sitting on the hoods or hanging off the axles like acrobats.

Inside a tall, curving, templelike structure, people place mementos, photographs, messages to people, all intended to go up in flames in a fire ceremony.

This is Burning Man, an annual festival held in the middle of a desert in northwestern Nevada. Every year, people descend upon the empty space and construct a temporary city called Black Rock City, full of art installations and gifted food and experiences. At the end of the week, there is a symbolic burn ceremony, where a large effigy is lit on fire.

Burning Man is a massive event with its own subculture, and many of its art installations, happenings, and performances fall under the "immersive" umbrella. It is a source of inspiration for many, and its influence is felt in the Bay Area and beyond the entire year, beyond the bounds of the single festival.

San Francisco in the late seventies and early-to-mid eighties was an epicenter for people exploring the ways that people could play in spaces.

A group known as the Suicide Club[*] was formed by several friends

---

[*] Please note: no suicide was actually involved. The group was named for a collection of short detective stories by Robert Louis Stevenson about adventure seekers who stumble upon a secret society.

interested in the idea of group creativity: Gary Warne, who owned the used-paperback bookstore Circus of the Soul, and Adrienne Burk, David Warren, and Nancy Prussia.

They recruited members through a newsletter for the "Communiversity" that was headquartered in Circus of the Soul, part of an education-reform movement that aimed to make education free, collaborative, and community-supported.

Their ad read:

Charter Member Meeting of the SF Suicide Club

Meeting regularly but at odd times.

Members must agree to set their worldly affairs in order, to enter into the REAL world of chaos, cacaphony [sic] and dark saturnalia, and they must further agree to live each day as though it were their last, for it may BE. The club will explore untravelled, exotic, dasmal [sic] and exhilarating experiences of life: deserted cemeteries, storms, caving, haunted houses, Nazi bars, fanatical movements, hot air ballooning, stunts, expose, impersonation. The Club will be ongoing for the rest of our lives.

Nancy Prussia, Gary Warne, Adrienne Burk, David Warren, R.J. Mololepozy, The Phantom, The Crimson Pirate, Nancy Drew & The Hardy Boys.

Notably, the Communiversity had originally been part of a curriculum at San Francisco State University, but they parted ways after SFSU wouldn't approve a class on practical jokes.

Any member of the Suicide Club could propose events, which included pranks (for example, riding cable cars in the nude), climbing bridges, offering literary tours, putting on treasure hunts, exploring abandoned industrial spaces, and other "planned chaos."

This type of good-humored anarchy would inform several movements that followed, and its attitude persists to this day.

The Cacophony Society and Urban Exploration

In 1986, former members of the Suicide Club formed the Cacophony Society. It is, in spirit, very similar to the Suicide Club: there are field trips, performance-art shows, educational workshops, and pranks.

While the previous organization, in their own words, was "neither secretive nor publicity-seeking," chapters of the Cacophony Society find a bit of spectacle helpful in recruiting new members. They create costumed events, like the SantaCon, an annual holiday event, inspired by Danish performance art group Solvognen, in which people dressed as Santa Claus gather in public spaces to delight and confuse onlookers as they make merry. The rowdiness increases exponentially through the day as the group binge drinks and causes chaos in one giant red-and-white mass.

Burning Man

Burning Man is an annual event that takes place in the Black Rock Desert in Nevada, northeast of Reno—about a day's drive from San Francisco. It describes itself as not a festival but "a city wherein almost everything that happens is created entirely by its citizens, who are active participants in the experience."

Each year, people gather on the playa and erect a temporary city.

One of the principles of Burning Man is "Leave no trace." The event works with the Bureau of Land Management to ensure that every speck of trash is removed from the site once the city is disassembled and attendees have gone home.

Burning Man evolved from a solstice ritual on a San Francisco beach, and a Dadaist temporary "happening" organized by one of the founders of the Cacophony Society.

In its early years in the nineties, it was an event spread by word of mouth, often through Internet forums, to people who had never met in person before.

Unlike its medieval counterparts, however, Burning Man exists in opposition to commerce. First and foremost, people are supposed to be self-reliant, carrying everything in that they might need, including food, shelter, and water. Second, it is strictly a "gifting economy." No money is exchanged, and no reciprocal bartering is needed. People give freely, and people accept graciously.

Burning Man opened to the public in 1996 and attracted eight thousand attendees. (Today, it's more like fifty thousand.)

As the event—or rather, the population of the temporary city—grew, new restrictions had to be put in place to ensure attendee safety. For example, the setup was now designed around a grid, to allow emergency vehicles to gain quick access to residences.

The art and performance at Burning Man are part of this gifting. Artists spend months out of the year and their own personal funds to create the vehicles, sculptures, costumes, and installations that populate the city.

This spirit pervades the Bay Area, influencing other artists and immersive work in the region.

LONDON AND NEW YORK CITY

A group of people stand in a dark room. Most of them are wearing masks that cover their whole faces: white, eerie shapes that seem to come from another age, or maybe another world. The people are standing clustered around a claw-foot bathtub.

The crowd parts. A nurse ushers in a woman—both unmasked—and helps her take off her robe and step into the tub, fully nude. They completely ignore the masked audience; in the world of these characters, the audience simply does not exist.

The woman is shaking, visibly distraught. The nurse soothes her, then leaves the room to prepare some medicine.

In the tub, the woman rocks back and forth, mumbling to herself as her inner turmoil grows. She opens her hands to show that blood has appeared there, seemingly from nowhere. She looks around, and suddenly, she can see the people in masks. They were invisible just a moment ago. She shrieks, terrified, showing her bloody palms to the people, seemingly pleading for help.

The audience looks around. Before, they were invisible to one another as well, merely anonymous figures in the crowd shuffling around to get a better view of the action.

Are these people voyeurs, taking advantage of this naked, vulnerable woman by craning their necks to see her distress? Are they ghosts, floating around a space as the characters' lives play out in front of them, with neither side able to touch the other?

Under the terrified woman's gaze, the people in masks become suddenly all too tangible.

The nurse rushes back over, soothing the woman again. She calms down, and once more, the audience fades back into invisibility, mere shades of the imagination conjured in her panic.

The woman is Lady Macbeth, tormented with guilt after encouraging her husband to murder King Duncan, hallucinating the appearance of blood on her hands.

This is a scene from *Sleep No More*, a staging of the Shakespeare play *Macbeth* in New York City. It is set in a vaguely 1930s noir hotel (along with a graveyard, a forest, a village with a taxidermist and tailor, suites of rooms, and a hospital wing). The audience, wearing masks, moves freely around the set and amid the characters as the play is happening.

Productions of *Sleep No More* took place in London, England, and Brookline, Massachusetts, and the production found major success and a permanent home in New York City, allowing it to create another permanent venue in Shanghai, China.

The massive immersive set, intriguing and sexy stories, and ease of access has made *Sleep No More* a must-do experience for tourists and residents alike, and its popularity has changed the face of immersive theater.

Rave Culture and the Free-Party Movement

Raves emerged in the 1980s with the rise of electronic music, with people gathering in fields and homes to dance to music pumped out of speakers. In the early nineties in the United Kingdom, people often gathered in the countryside for these informal weekend events, free from the restrictions of city-based club scenes.

"Free parties" were one such type of gathering, held outdoors or in abandoned buildings, with no entrance fee for participants. While many raves and festivals were commercial events, since the 1970s, free parties had embraced the autonomy of their attendees, asking people to contribute to event setup and using the motto "The best thing is to bring what you expect to find."[1]

In 1974, a free festival took place at Stonehenge, and when it was over, about thirty of the attendees remained in the fields nearby, camping in tents and a geodesic dome, a precursor to Britain's subculture of "new age travelers," people who lived on the road, camped at festivals, and embraced anti-capitalism and environmental sustainability.

Writing in *Festival Eye* magazine, an author named Krystoff described the evolution of this subculture and its connection to the free-festival scene:

> *The Free City of Camden, which became the base for early Stonehenge festivals, was a loose, street-by-street network of squatters, revolutionaries and artists who subscribed to the philosophy of giving and practiced consensus politics rather than "representative democracy," establishing an anarchic lifestyle and a sense of community feeling. The first festivals at Stonehenge were the expression of this kind of community feeling. They were spontaneous "happenings" and quickly attracted other avant-garde groups and communes from around the country. The eviction of the Free City of Camden made tens of thousands of people homeless and many of them took to the road. The festival became the community's home, rather than its playground.*[2]

With easily transportable speakers and equipment, electronic music known as "acid house"—thanks to the community's general love of psychedelic drugs—became a major feature at free parties, at least until a 1994 government declaration allowing police to shut down any event with music characterized by "the emission of a succession of repetitive beats."

Glastonbury and Lost Vagueness

The Glastonbury Festival was originally conceived in the 1970s as an easy-to-access, hippie-friendly festival, heavily inspired by the free-party movement and featuring spontaneous entertainment, music, dance, and performance in the spirit of medieval festivals.

During the eighties, attendance grew by tens of thousands every year. In the nineties, Glastonbury underwent major growing pains after a clash between security guards and new age travelers camping alongside the festival resulted in a riot with hundreds of arrests.[3]

Traveler Roy Gurvitz, who picked up part-time work at Glastonbury when he visited each year, acted as a go-between for festival officials and people in the new age travelers camp, proposing an in-festival event: an "ironic faux casino" dubbed Lost Vagueness.

In the southeast corner of the festival, an area was designated for a small casino, café, and tent. The revelers donned ball gowns and tuxedos, and an "anti-society DIY debauchery" art scene was born.

Lost Vagueness lasted until 2007. It had tripled in size, and as any project involving people grows, the safety needs and logistics grow alongside it. The organization who ran it had begun producing paid corporate events as a side gig, and the event reached a breaking point: it either had to evolve or dissolve.

So, dissolve it did. Gurvitz left, and the event was replaced by Shangri-La, produced by many of the same original team.

"It's slick, well organised and doesn't feel like everybody's about to get squashed," said producer Leila Jones of the new party area in a 2018 *Guardian* interview.

Carnival and other masquerade revelries offer people a chance to change their identities. A mask is powerful: it disguises identity and social class, and it allows its wearer to act out behaviors they may not otherwise feel free to engage in.

The "Bauta" is the most famous of these masks. It covers the entire face, and has a pointy chin that allows its wearer to eat, drink, and speak without the need to remove it.

In Venice, the government regulated the use of these masks.

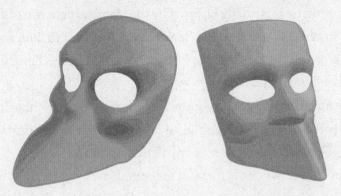

The *Sleep No More* mask and a traditional Bauta mask

This sense of possibility, with perhaps a whiff of danger, is a powerful emotion in the right designer's hands. This feeling is at the core of the work produced by Punchdrunk, the theater company from London that created *Sleep No More*.

The company was founded in 2000 by Felix Barrett, who was inspired by unusual venues.

In *Sleep No More*, there is no stage—the building itself is the performance space, and the audience may roam more or less freely. In a typical stage play, a character might come onstage, deliver their line, and then disappear. Not so for these shows. There is no offstage. Instead, a character might enter a scene, hand someone a letter, and then go to a shop, meet someone for a lover's tryst, or go back to their own room to look sadly at a set of nostalgic photographs. And this is the case for every character in the play.

Audience members can choose their path through these scenes. Do they stay and watch the person who received the letter as they read it and compose a reply? Do they follow the letter deliverer out of the room and into their next scene? Do they go the opposite direction, wandering until they find something else that interests them? All these are valid options in this play and in this theater space.

This design was partially inspired by the team's experience of attending raves in the UK, which were often secretive, difficult to find, and held in strange, out-of-the-way locales, with sometimes-incorrect instructions scrawled on photocopied maps.

In theater, there's a concept known as the "fourth wall." Imagine this as an invisible barrier between the audience and the actors onstage (or between the readers or viewers of any fictional work).

When an actor or character talks to the audience, or mentions being a character in a book or a movie, this is called "breaking the fourth wall." In play versions of the story of Peter Pan, he turns to the audience and asks for them to applaud, to save Tinker Bell; this is an example of breaking the fourth wall.

(I am breaking the fourth wall by addressing you directly, right now. Spoooky.)

In theater, the audience obviously knows that they're watching a show. This is what we call "suspension of disbelief," a term that has become increasingly more relevant to these types of entertainment. Meanwhile, the actors behave as if they're "real," going through the motions of their own lives, thoughts, and dreams.

Punchdrunk shows take inspiration from a genre known as "site-sympathetic theater" or "environmental theater," which is any kind of production that is performed in a location that is not a standard theater with a stage, proscenium, and curtains.

The audience may still be seated, pointed at the action. If actors move throughout a seated audience, that may be called "interactive theater," and if the audience moves through the space, it may be called "promenade theater."

This is all just to say there are a lot of ways to experiment with how an audience watches and interacts with a performance.

Several other innovative immersive performances emerged in London during the same period. In 2004, a production called *You Me Bum Bum Train*, created by Morgan Lloyd and Kate Bond, moved unprepared but willing participants through a variety of surprising scenes. Sometimes they were asked to crowd-surf, to give a speech at a wedding backed by a church choir that sang the words they said, or to interview an actual celebrity on a fake talk show.

In 2007, Fabien Riggall founded Secret Cinema, an interactive film-screening event. Participants are invited to dress in costumes from the world of the movie and watch themed live performances and music. Some productions include large-scale environmental build-outs, such as the town from *Back to the Future* or the cyberpunk streets of *Blade Runner*.

The immersive theater world owes a huge debt to *Sleep No More* for pioneering this new form of promenade theater. The show is site-specific, as it responds to and takes over unconventional spaces, like hotels and warehouses. It requires the audience to suspend their disbelief as they move through the space. And it also has moments of interaction. It's a type of breaking the fourth wall—suddenly, the characters recognize the presence of the audience members. However, the characters don't acknowledge that they are a part of our world, within the construct of the play. Instead, the audience member becomes a part of the character's world. They are part of this living, breathing fiction that surrounds them.

When we talk about "immersion," this is usually what we're referring to. People want to be entertained. They are eager and willing to suspend their disbelief. And it's also pretty fun to escape the real world for a while.

Even better when that world is a secret to everyone around us, and only we, the chosen few, are granted access to it.

So when a work of art invites us to all that, and more, to actually become a part of that world, even for a little bit of time . . . that is pretty wonderful. And that feeling has formed the foundation of much of experiential arts and culture since the invention and popularization of a radical new piece of technology: the Internet.

CHAPTER 8

The 1990s–2000s:
The Dot-Com Era and Beyond

This is not a game.

—*A.I. ARTIFICIAL INTELLIGENCE* MOVIE TRAILER (2001)

In the early 2000s, the world was experiencing the end of the first "dot-com boom," but our relationship with the Internet and its storytelling possibilities was still going strong.

Think about *The Matrix*—in that film, characters are hackers who only know one another by their online handles. There's a sense of mystery and a little bit of danger behind meeting the person behind the screen name, but the people are united by their mutual addiction to exploring the strange, remote corners of the web.

The Internet at the time was a promise of a world where all human knowledge would be easily accessible. Any book, movie, or song could be digitized, shared, and experienced. If you wanted to share your art or photography, you could create your own space—a "home" page—with no limits to self-expression.

It also promised that you could find community in these far reaches.

So, naturally, up sprang a game genre that took advantage of these feelings. The idea that behind every corner, a game could be waiting, a story layered over the real world—who could resist that?

This was the era of alternate reality games (ARGs), adventure stories that combined online puzzles with in-person meetups and adventures.

SUSPENSION OF DISBELIEF

The sky is trickling rain, a drizzle that's uncomfortable, but not so uncomfortable that it stops a group of friends from gathering around a pay phone.

One of them keeps checking their watch.

They appear to be waiting for something.

Suddenly, the pay phone rings.

The friends look at one another, and someone reaches forward, picking up the receiver from its cradle before it can ring again. They hold it to their ear.

"Hello?"

A robotic voice asks, "Crew member, what is your nickname?"

"Operator," the person replies.

A brief exchange, and the task is complete. They put the phone receiver back in the cradle, and the friends turn to one another with big grins on their faces.

"The axon is unlocked," someone says. "Let's get back to a computer."

At a different location, at a different time, another pay phone rings. This time, there's only one person waiting there to answer it.

"Hello," they say.

"Hello, Operator," the voice says, quizzing the person. "What special skills can you contribute?"

"Uh, I can play my guitar," the person replies. "It's in the trunk of my car."

"Put the phone down and get your guitar," the voice demands.

The only sounds transmitted are a heavy *clunk* as the receiver is put down on the edge of the pay phone, still connected, and the pitter-patter of footsteps running away into the distance.

Agonizing minutes later, the footsteps approach again. The person has retrieved his guitar and is ready to play. He strums part of "Wish You Were Here."

On the other end of the phone, the "puppet masters," or "game control," are silently cheering as they listen in.

This is an actual scenario from I Love Bees, an alternate reality game that ran in 2004, part of a viral marketing campaign to promote the video game Halo 2.

The team would complete hundreds of these scheduled calls, ringing pay phones all over the United States.

Each phone call was a part of the game, forming a grid of "nodes" that players had to unlock. They knew that when enough calls were completed, they would be given clues to the next puzzle. The players had to coordinate across the country to find people in the right locations to answer each incoming call.

These games provide an alternate reality: a layer of story on top of the real world, and an in-between place where people know that they're playing a game but also opt in to a suspension of disbelief. The lines between the game and your real life begin to blur, and you're able to look at the once-familiar world in an entirely new way.

Imagine that you're walking down the street, passing a pay phone. (If you're of a certain age, anyway—pay phones aren't really around much these days. Just pretend, for now.)

So you're passing this pay phone, and it rings. You answer it, naturally. But something strange happens—the person on the other end of the line knows your name and has a personal message for you: there's a mystery, and only you can solve it.

How did they know your name? How did they know what number to call? How did they know you would be there, at that exact moment?

This concept of blurring the lines between a game and your real life is part of the inspiration for alternate reality games.

ARGs are a mix of story, theater, role-playing, puzzle-solving, and community forming. They are usually created to promote a film, game, or other property. The obviousness of the marketing can vary between extreme subtlety and more obvious stories that are set in the world of the film being promoted.

And ARG design draws from a mix of puzzle-heavy, public-facing game design and challenges.

In the 1840s, Edgar Allan Poe ran cryptographic contests in magazines, asking readers to submit their most advanced ciphers in an attempt to stump him and challenging his readers in turn.

More than a century later, in the 1970s, at-home sleuths puzzled over armchair treasure hunts, books with puzzles woven into their illustrated pages. When solved correctly, the puzzles would lead to a real-world buried treasure.

People in the seventies also took to the streets for overnight puzzle games in the Bay Area and Seattle, driving between puzzle checkpoints in a race to the finish.

These city-size puzzle games inspired a 1997 movie, *The Game*, starring Michael Douglas, which in turn inspired more real-world puzzle events of increasing depth and complexity.

This world of story combined with puzzles found a dedicated audience online. When *The Blair Witch Project* was released in 1999, its realistic world-building made people wonder if the terrifying events of the film were actually true. And in 2001, online storytelling found a new, innovative form in an alternate reality game called The Beast.

THIS IS NOT A GAME

Edgar Allan Poe

American writer Edgar Allan Poe may be best known today for his famous poem "The Raven," and spooky stories like "The Tell-Tale Heart" and "The Cask of Amontillado," but in his day he was a prolific magazine writer.

In December 1839, he issued a challenge in *Alexander's Messenger*: submit a cipher, and he would solve it—or publish it, if he could not.

"We say again deliberately that human ingenuity cannot concoct a cypher which human ingenuity cannot resolve," he wrote.

He received roughly one hundred submissions, and published the results of many of his favorites.

In August 1841, he published a cryptogram in *Graham's Magazine*, promising a year's subscription to anyone who could solve it:[1]

£ 7i A itagi niinbiiit thitvuiaib9g h auehbiif b ivgiht itau ⟶
gvuiitiif 4 t$bt2ihtbo £iiiadb9 iignit £d i2 ta5ta whbo ttbibtiii†it9
A iti if X hti 4 ithtt ⟶ i‡ bnniathubii iSt b eaovuhoSu vtt7diboif*
iti nihd6Xht na3ig an choo$ht u‡tnvotigg2 iibtvo$ifb Eaovu£avg

iinoht$h7 niau iti vtheiigbo iit6 A itagi t7iitig h fifvti iti gvugidvti
bubodbub9 A tiiiiaditiavg nbttg iStavi fvuhiiu £thnhiti niiiit8 †
bni 4 iiu£$i ht d£bo evodbiSa ‡ nbiivihiti uavtib£g ibei—it
dbuvo$if ia niafvti uvgtvnvobi buai9g uii iti £giSv9 i2 gvuiiti A
uu iiubisg ibg tai—it iStavi tbvgi iti itiui A i2 intiuiiibo taovutg
an dvaihfh¶ iavitbog ¶f a itivghbgight ittauh$h7g ht t7eiigb9bo
£iiitavigi.

(If you don't feel like solving that, you can read the answer in the
"Solutions" section at the end of this book.)

In 1979, an unassuming illustrator, Kit Williams, released a book that
would go on to influence a generation of puzzle makers.

The book was *Masquerade*. Its pages are filled with illustrations of detailed pastoral scenes, with hillsides, animals, and people in festive clothing. It was immensely popular upon release and inspired the genre we
now call "armchair treasure hunts."

The book begins: "To solve the hidden riddle, you must use your
eyes, / And find the hare in every picture that may point you to the prize."

On every page, there is a hidden image of a hare. The illustrations are
sprinkled with other puzzles, and each illustration has a border around it
that contains a rhyme or a riddle. For example, on page 1: "I am as cold as
earth / as old **as** earth / and in the earth am I / one of six to eight."

Let's break down this puzzle.

In the sentence, several of the letters are painted red (made bold
here), while others have small marks as part of their makeup. The red letters spell "hare," while the marked letters spell "golden."

The riddle refers to being buried, so it can perhaps be concluded that
it's referring to the treasure, which was buried. "One of six to eight" is

likely a reference to King Henry VIII's wives, specifically Catherine of Aragon, who was banished to Ampthill Castle—near the location of the treasure, in Ampthill, Bedfordshire.

There's one final, deeply hidden set of clues, which is found using a method described circuitously in another illustration. It involves drawing lines from the eyes of animals in the illustrations to letters in the border, to spell out an additional word.

On the first page, this word is "Catherines." This is part of the larger puzzle of the book, with each page resulting in one word, to form a complete sentence pointing at the buried treasure.

Masquerade was eventually solved, but the finding of its treasure, a golden hare, was controversial. Two teachers correctly solved the puzzle and excavated dirt in the correct location. The hare was in the dirt, but the teachers missed it, and went home, thinking they had gotten the answer wrong.

The hare was then found in the dirt remnant and claimed by a friend of the author's ex-girlfriend, using her inside knowledge about the location of the burial.

Funnily enough, the hare went on its own mysterious journey. It was later used as collateral to start a game software company, and when that company was liquidated, the hare was sold at a Sotheby's auction for £31,900.

After the book was published, Williams withdrew from the public eye, but after the auction he spoke out publicly against the find.

Since then, there has been a semiregular stream of armchair treasure hunts, based around published books with illustrations, photography, and poems.

Puzzle Hunts

The ARG genre is also rooted in puzzle hunts, overnight events that send teams on long journeys, solving puzzles and completing challenges along the way.

In 1973, graphic designer Donald Luskin and his friend Patrick Carlyle ran a game for friends that they called the Game, a car-based chase around the city. This inspired a Disney movie, *Midnight Madness*, released in 1980.

In *Midnight Madness* eccentric graduate student Leon runs an all-night game for five students and their teams. They drive all around the city, completing tasks and solving puzzles.

Inspired by the movie, in 1985, high schooler Joe Belfiore created an all-night puzzle race for his friends, like the one in the film. These games ran in the Bay Area for years, until Belfiore moved to Seattle to take a job at Microsoft, bringing the Game with him.

Around this time, another puzzle hunt was founded in Boston, Massachusetts: the MIT Mystery Hunt. In 1981, on the campus of the Massachusetts Institute of Technology (MIT), groups of students gathered to solve twelve clues and ciphers. In the following years, the number of participants grew and the hunt became more and more complicated.

Today, it's not uncommon for the hunt to last a full weekend, beginning on Friday night and wrapping up on Sunday night, with teams made of hundreds of people solving puzzles simultaneously.

The MIT Mystery Hunt inspired similar hunts by other organizations and institutions, including Microsoft in Seattle and Stanford in California.

Throughout the eighties, the chain of inspiration continued, with yet another movie taking its cues from all-night puzzle games.

The Game with Michael Douglas

The Game is a thriller that was released in 1997. In it, investment banker Nicholas Van Orton struggles with the approach of his forty-eighth birthday, as his father killed himself on his own forty-eighth birthday. Nicholas feels a looming sense of trepidation as he passes time alone in his empty mansion.

His semi-estranged younger brother, Conrad, gifts him with a personalized game that begins with an intensive physical checkup and psychological profile.

As Nicholas goes about his everyday life, he begins to overhear people mentioning things related to the game. But as time goes on, the lines between his real life and the game begin to blur in more serious and dangerous ways.

The Game perfectly captures the thrill and appeal of ARGs. Imagine being handed a note by a stranger on the street. You open it and to your surprise, it's customized for you, sending you off to meet a stranger, solve a code, or see an amazing performance.

It's all about a call to adventure that could change your life—if you're willing to answer when it comes knocking at your door.

The Blair Witch Project

When *The Blair Witch Project* came out in 1999, nobody was sure if it was real or not.

The Blair Witch Project is a "found footage" film. It was filmed on a very tight budget, so the filmmakers leaned into the aesthetic of hand-held cameras and rough editing, using the framing story to explain the deliberately amateurish technique.

They auditioned film students for the roles, and sent them out into the woods with food, camping supplies, and cameras. They would leave further instructions for filming their improvised scenes, and at night would sneak up to the camp to provide events and scares for the actors to react to.

The film opens with a statement that it was put together using footage recovered from a group of hiking filmmakers who had gone missing.

Nothing about the footage, or the way that it is edited, suggests that it is anything but real. The camera is shaky, there are plenty of scenes of people goofing off, and as the tension and horror of the film increase, they speak directly into the camera, recording final messages that they hope will reach their families.

And the marketing around the film supported this illusion. The production created missing person posters for the actors, who went by their real names in the film. They also created a fictional, though real-seeming, documentary featuring interviews with police and investigators, and the film's website provided additional "evidence" of newspaper clippings and missing person reports.

The marketing helped support this aura of mystery, and it created a great sense of intrigue.

The *Chicago Tribune* declared it "the first Internet movie," quoting one of the film's distributors, who said it appealed to "a young Internet audience out there that hasn't been tapped. . . . This movie converges with that audience. They've embraced it. All the kids have seen it on the Internet."[2]

The Beast

Many people love a good mystery, and there's a certain personality that would love to be swept into an adventure via secret, clandestine note or hidden sign. (I count myself among them.)

In 2001, a group of those people found one another, thanks to the

Internet and the first ARG, a game known as The Beast, created to promote the Steven Spielberg movie *A.I. Artificial Intelligence.*

Now, there were certainly precursors to this example, as with all inventions. But The Beast was so influential to every game that came after it that we can point to it as the original.

There were three "rabbit holes," or points of entry into the game, a term that refers to Alice, the girl who visits Wonderland when she follows a white rabbit into its hole under a hedge.

Each rabbit hole was a way to introduce people to the fictional world of The Beast, which was set several years after the events taking place in the film. One movie trailer featured a hidden phone number that led to a fictional character's voice mail. This character, Dr. Jeanine Salla, was also credited in movie posters as a "sentient machine therapist." And finally, promotional posters contained hidden codes referring to a murder mystery.

The game introduced elements of the fictional film into the physical world, treating them as nonfiction. At a Q & A session featuring *A.I. Artificial Intelligence* cast and crew, they were asked about their experience working with Dr. Salla—who, again, is not a real person, although they answered the question as if she were.[3]

The community of The Beast puzzle solvers, who called themselves Cloudmakers, tracked every mention of the game, hunting for these clues hidden in plain sight. The creators of the game also remained responsive to the players, making new story lines and shifting plot points based on their activity and interests. Things that players wrote in their investigations would appear in the game or on in-world websites.

The lines between real life and the world of the game were blurred, and people loved it.

———

I love ARGs because they're ephemeral. The experience of playing them is one of collaborating with a group of people who have gathered together, in real time, to tackle challenges.

And the stories respond to players' action—in one game I played, a character was supposed to be killed off, but players managed to intervene, leaving voice mails and sending emails to the character's friends. The game designers decided to let them live.

I love this dance between player and creator, a unique experience that's only possible because of the people who are participating, right there and then.

But ARGs are often short-lived, and as marketing promotions they tend to rise and fall in popularity, the victim of fluctuating advertising budgets. (That said, there are often one or two running, if you search for them—check out the Recommended Reading section of this book for some places to look.)

One thing that remains, however, is the community of puzzle solvers that comes together to play these games.

When I played, I grew incredibly close to the people in the ARG community. After all, we were spending hours every day chatting, not just about the games but about our lives, too. I know many people who met their future spouse through these games.

In fact, I'm one of them!

CHAPTER 9

The 2000s: Precursors and the Birth of Escape Rooms

You are standing in an open field west of a white house,
with a boarded front door. There is a small mailbox here.
—OPENING LINES TO THE TEXT ADVENTURE ZORK, 1980

In 2004, one of the hottest things online was an unassuming game with simple graphics in primary colors.

Crimson Room, a Flash game created by developer Toshimitsu Takagi, struck a chord with its point-and-click interaction style and just-hard-enough puzzles.

Its popularity reflected a hunger for new types of gameplay and experiences. The online Crimson Room series and its imitators inspired the creation of real-world puzzle games in cities all over the world.

There are three interactive, puzzle-like experiences that are responsible for the creation of an entire industry of escape rooms. They share the same DNA—a desire for adventure and giving people the gift of experience, and a love of puzzles—but are each fundamentally different in very interesting ways.

In October 2004, in the United States, a company called 5 Wits opened a guided adventure inspired by theme parks, which put the patron at the center of a playful experience.

In 2007, *SCRAP*, a free magazine in Kyoto, Japan, ran a puzzle game event to go alongside an article about online escape games, spawning a puzzle empire.

And in 2011, in Budapest, Hungary, a team-building coordinator realized that he could evoke a state of "flow" in small teams who were placed inside specially designed adventures.

These three companies laid the groundwork that all future escape rooms would build upon.

VIRAL SPREAD

Text flashes across the screen, white letters on a black background: "I have to escape."

The player clicks, reading the scenario: a person drank too much and has woken up locked in a strange room. They don't recognize it and have no memory of how they got there.

Clicking some more, the player sees that the room has red walls and ceilings, yellow furniture, and a blue door.

A few more clicks around the room reveal that some objects will react: the corner of a pillow lifts up when touched, revealing a golden key.

A drawer that was previously locked opens when the key is used on it, giving the player a power cord.

And so on, until finally the player solves enough steps to uncover a screwdriver to use on the room's doorknob, allowing them to escape into a black void.

This game is what we now consider the first digital escape room: 2004's Crimson Room by Toshimitsu Takagi. Describing itself as "an interactive game that you escape from . . . using your idea[s] and your inspiration," the game's colorful, blocky imagery conceals the trickiness of its clever puzzles.

It was built in Adobe Flash, a multimedia software platform that was popular during the first "dot-com boom," and was a big hit upon release.

The Crimson Room inspired hundreds of similar games, in addition to several official sequels. This genre of games, known as Takagism in honor of its creator, introduced the concept of a locked room demanding escape to a large audience of online game players.

Between other popular early Internet topics such as flash mobs, raves, Burning Man, alternate reality games, Punchdrunk, *The Matrix*, and Crimson Room, the public consciousness was full to the brim with interactive, theatrical, and puzzle-filled experiences and media.

It seems only natural, then, that someone eventually had the brilliant idea: What if that type of puzzle game was set in a *real life, actual room*?

5 Wits

An illustrated storybook comes to life, as if by magic, its pictures moving on the pages in front of you.

A lyrical voice fills the room: A dragon has escaped, and a princess is asking for your help. Will you be the one to answer the call?

Of course you will!

You explore a castle, finding its many hidden secrets.

Nearby, a child reaches up high to insert a key into a lock underneath a glowing Celtic knot. They turn it, and the knot turns green—success.

A bookcase springs open, revealing a chamber with a royal throne. In the king's chamber, your group is faced with more riddles: here, you must put shields into cubbies in the right order to unlock the next challenge.

Later, the throne slides to the side, revealing a secret passageway.

Can you discover the castle's secrets and rescue the dragon? Or will you end up feeling the heat of its flames?

This is a 5 Wits adventure, an interactive experience in a highly decorated set.

They opened their doors in 2004, well before the first formal "escape rooms."

Inspired by theme park environmental design, they share the same immersive DNA, desiring to provide a thoughtful, adventurous experience to people.

5 Wits is another early entry in the United States "interactive experience" scene. Its creator, Matthew DuPlessie, was a student at MIT, studying mechanical engineering. Between his junior and senior years, he had what he described as a "terrible" summer internship.

"It was one of those where you're in a cubicle that's six feet wide," he said. "Computers were slow. [We were] doing 3D modeling on a computer, and we would actually have two in our cubicle. And you had to roll from one to the other because you'd click to make it change on one screen, and it would take the computer three minutes to actually execute the change. So you'd roll over and work on another computer for those three minutes."

DuPlessie thought that there must be something more fun that he could do with an engineering degree, and with a friend's help, decided on theme parks.

"Probably most engineers at some point in their life say, 'Oh, I want to build roller coasters,'" DuPlessie said. "I was not into roller coasters or that kind of theme park stuff, in terms of the rides. But I love the environments; I love the spaces that they created. So my buddy and I found the IAAPA trade show that year."

IAAPA is the International Association of Amusement Parks and Attractions. DuPlessie said that in 1998, the event was for industry people, and students didn't normally attend, so the show had no way to label them, except as "buyers."

"This is the industry-insiders show for the theme park world," he said. "Everything from the guys who designed and built roller coasters to cotton candy vendor's machines, and everything in between, including companies that specialize in the concept design and the thematic design of these environments. So at this trade show, I essentially walked around and had a hundred miniature interviews over the course of a couple of days."

DuPlessie and his friend both found jobs via that trade show. He began working for a company called Living Color in Florida, working on projects like Disney's Animal Kingdom Lodge, a 1,400-room hotel in Orlando, Florida.

He started as a project engineer, working under project managers and leads. But when the leads on his team quit, he was promoted, last minute, because he was the only one who knew anything about the project. Suddenly, he found himself managing that project for the next year and a half, learning construction, themed entertainment, and how to dress a space. When he left his job, his boss made him promise to stay in touch.

Next, he attended Harvard Business School in Boston, Massachusetts, from 2001 to 2003.

"I started writing, each night, a business plan for what became 5 Wits," DuPlessie said. "And the thinking was, nobody's going to give a kid three billion dollars to open his own Disney World; I can't do it at that scale. So how can I shrink a theme park experience? That's where I was coming from."

Over the next two years, the concept took shape for a one-off, retail store–size themed environment. They chose the theme of an Ancient Egyptian pharaoh's tomb.

Once the general plan was in place, the next decisions were about what the theme park industry refers to as "throughput," the number of people who get through an attraction on a given day or in a certain amount of time.

Generally speaking, the more people that you can quickly move through a space, the more money you can make, because you can sell more tickets. In a theme park, it means shorter lines for rides.

If the experience is short, the ticket price may need to be lower, and if the designer is trying to tell a story, the visitor may need more time in the experience, so the throughput and ticket price need to be adjusted to match.

Throughput in theme parks is maximized by having staggered starts to an experience, which means multiple groups are inside an attraction at the same time, in a continuous line.

Some examples of throughput:

A carousel has a low throughput, because fifteen to sixty people load onto it, ride the carousel for two to three minutes, and then disembark before the next group can get on. This is true for escape rooms, too, where two to eight people play a game for an hour and must complete it before the next group can begin.

Attractions like It's a Small World at Disneyland are known as "interval loaders." For It's a Small World, up to twenty-four people climb into a boat, which takes off on a track, traveling through the attraction's scenes for a fifteen-minute experience. While those boats are inside the attraction, other boats are finishing up and loading new people in.

It's a Small World can, in theory, move two thousand people through in an hour, although that doesn't take into account real-life logistics like delays, or boats being sent without passengers to keep the ride flowing.

Many haunted houses also operate using interval loading, as they have vignette scenes or scares that quickly "reset" each time a new group passes through. The interval prevents a group behind another from running into another group of people or seeing a scare too early, which would spoil the surprise.

A large haunted house can last for thirty to sixty minutes, and an operation that sends groups of four to eight through at thirty- or forty-five-second intervals can often move five hundred to one thousand people in an hour.

The Haunted Mansion at Disneyland is a "continuous loader," with as many cars on the track as possible. The ride moves slowly, to give people time to climb into the cars, which hold groups of three. Because it is dark inside the attraction, and because the cars turn to face important story scenes, the presence of other riders isn't distracting to the experience.

The Haunted Mansion experience lasts nine minutes, and roughly three thousand people can go through it in an hour, for a potential total of forty-two thousand riders in a day. The average daily attendance at Disney parks is between fifty thousand and sixty-five thousand, so that's a big chunk of visitors.

For 5 Wits, the throughput question drove the design.

DuPlessie recalled the questions he asked himself at the time. "Is it just a spectacle to look at? If it's that tiny, the duration of the stay is going to be so short that people aren't going to want to spend money on it, and we have to have a reasonable ticket price to stay viable. So how can we increase the duration of the experience?"

He also wanted visitors to be able to participate as a first-person adventure, because of his love of games and puzzles. And he attributes his decision to make the experience narrative to his experience working on Disney projects.

"It was obvious a story needed to be written," he said. "It needed to have a narrative that drew people through the whole thing, the puzzles needed to make sense within the context of that Egyptian tomb environment. And you basically had a little team game."

DuPlessie entered his business plan into the school's competition, but it was eliminated in the first round. The venture capitalist judges were seeking the next Google or Apple, a company that could grow to reach a billion dollars in sales. But DuPlessie's adviser, who taught his entrepreneurship class, thought the idea could be successful, and invested in the company.

DuPlessie's former boss from Living Color also invested, and brought in a third partner. Collectively, they contributed $650,000. From June 2003 to October 2004, DuPlessie worked to design and build the experience in Boston.

"There were no escape rooms to base it on," he said. "My references were more from the theme park world, the location-based attraction world, the larping world, from the haunted house world. It was just like: *What would work here?*"

He pointed out that 5 Wits adventures are different from escape rooms. To start, they're thirty to fifty minutes long and have a guide who goes with the group, keeping the game flowing and directing the narrative as people solve puzzles.

The rooms are designed for kids as well, so the puzzles aren't as difficult as some escape rooms, which are usually designed for adults.

"It's much more like playing through a movie in a very detailed, high-level set," he said. "It's much more of a themed attraction where you're playing through and solving puzzles in a group. There was never a locked door."

The original Tomb averaged forty-five minutes in length. The experience began at an archaeological dig site that led through a cave entrance and contained three sequential rooms in the tomb, built in just over two thousand square feet.

The company started a branch to design themed attractions for museums, theme parks, and other clients, and in 2010 opened a second location in Foxboro, Massachusetts.

In their newer locations, 5 Wits has created fully automated shows—a major innovation for venue-based entertainment.

"There is no staff member who goes with you," DuPlessie said. "All of our games are built to be fully self-resetting. Our current typical model is like a full-room adventure that takes half an hour, but we're starting a new group about every twelve minutes."

Also exciting is that the content of the attraction is regulated automatically based on how the group is performing. If the group does well, more plot points might be added, and if they're going slowly, they might receive a shorter version of a voiceover to keep the groups moving forward at the correct pace.

ParaPark

Players stand in a strange room with a curved ceiling and peeling paint.

The room is full of things, but they're not sure what to do.

Tentatively, someone reaches out, picking up a trash can and opening it. There are papers with codes inside, and the group smiles.

"This is it!" someone calls out, excited. Across the room, their teammate is opening a cabinet, which reveals a set of industrial lights, flickering with a pattern.

They progress through the room, exploring its secrets. Panels flip open on a big set of shelves, revealing more puzzles, clues, and things to solve.

The players race to complete puzzles, opening secret panels behind the wall, fiddling with the lock on a briefcase, trying to get into a locked safe.

In the corner, a timer counts down, but they're so engrossed in their game that they don't notice the minutes passing.

The team completes the final puzzle with seconds to spare, emerging with big, triumphant grins on their faces.

This is ParaPark, one of the first "formal" escape rooms in the world generally, and in Europe specifically.

Its creator, trained in team building and interested in evoking a state of "flow," pioneered a genre that would find its way to countries around the world.

In Budapest, Hungary, social worker Attila Gyurkovics needed a change.

He had moved from working with clients to focusing on team building and coaching for his fellow social workers. And as he began helping people deal with the functional problems that arise in the workplace, he realized that the concept could be expanded.

"I realized this concept could work, because I learned about group dynamics," he said. "What is a smaller group? Why do they work well and more efficiently together?"

The pieces fell into place when he learned about flow theory, named by Mihaly Csikszentmihalyi in 1975.

Flow theory is about the state of being "in the zone," or when a person is totally immersed in what they're doing. They are completely focused on their actions, their actions feel effortless, and they are performing the actions successfully.

The six factors of being "in flow," identified by Csikszentmihalyi and Jeanne Nakamura:

Intense and focused concentration on the present moment

Merging of action and awareness

A loss of reflective self-consciousness

A sense of personal control or agency over the situation or activity

A distortion of temporal experience; one's subjective experience of time is altered

Experience of the activity as intrinsically rewarding, also referred to as autotelic experience

Gyurkovics figured that it would be fun and interesting to introduce this into his work.

"Flow theory was really important in my concept," he said. "And also, I needed to figure out what to do in my life. I like motorbikes and do kickboxing. Adventure was an important thing to me. I was looking for that flow feeling. That loss of the self, forgetting everyday little things. Time seems fast or slow, distorted."

He knew he could apply the skills he had built up doing social work and team building with coworkers to a larger audience.

"I realized it's really important to give people adventure," he said. "Real adventure, not just a promise and something shiny or surface-level. You see advertising for new movies and think it's going to be great, but you watch it and you think, *I saw that already*. And you forget it as you leave it."

Digital puzzle games like Crimson Room helped guide his design sensibilities, introducing him to interlinked puzzle games as he learned a new language.

"I started to play hidden-object mystery games on the computer to practice English," he said. "In these point-and-click games, you need to explore your surroundings, you find something, you realize you can go to the other room of the castle, and so on. And I realized it could work in real life."

Gyurkovics had fond memories of exploring unknown places as a child and thought there was a viable business plan to be built on that feeling.

"The basic premise is, people together exploring an unknown place," he said. "Not just unknown, but a little bit weird. The tasks are to check in the wardrobe, see what's in the box, check what's on the computer. I studied the idea from every angle, with the flow theory and group-dynamic stuff. I realized it could work, it can be a great activity."

His experience organizing his coworkers informed his initial design.

"I decided it needed to be a group activity, and also a small-group activity, with maximum five, six, seven people," he said. "That's the optimal situation so that information doesn't disappear between people. There are problems with bigger groups when cliques form or people pick scapegoats. But in a small group, you can avoid all those problems."

And Gyurkovics realized that problem-solving tasks like those found in computer games could work in the real world.

"I had a moment when I realized it would work," he said. "Before this, I wasn't an entrepreneur, but when I realized it would work in real life, I realized I needed to at least try. I didn't make a business plan. I thought it would be in a bigger place, a whole house, where the groups spend half days. I fast realized I need to rent a whole house, do electricity, building, and construction."

The scale of the initial plan proved challenging, so he reconfigured the idea to fit available real estate.

"When I wanted to rent a big house, I realized in a half year, or three months, I'd run out of money," he said. "My brother actually said to me, if this concept will really work, then I need to make an example. So that's how I created the small rooms. I realized that I could find ruined cellars in cities and started with two or three small rooms in a game.

"I decided on the one-hour time frame and to make the whole game international, not relying on English," he added. "I realized it was lucky I chose that time framing. It's enough time to get involved in the activity but not for frustration to start in the group, or for group cohesion to weaken because people get tired."

The initial game was supposed to be a prototype to prove that the house-size experience would work, but it turned out that the smaller game was enough.

"That concept was so successful that it stuck," Gyurkovics said. "I started my small franchise network as well really quickly. The game was immediately popular, and word of mouth spread."

The location of the game was a great boost to business, too.

"We opened in July and didn't even have a website until September," he said. "Part of the building was a hostel, part was a bar. It was a great complex."

In the 2010s, Hungary experienced a financial crisis, which drove down prices in its property market. Rents became very affordable, with many prewar buildings in need of repair.

In Budapest's city center, many buildings were empty or unused because they were too expensive to renovate. So a trend arose of *romkoc-sma*, or "ruin bars," pubs that opened in abandoned and broken-down spaces, especially the historic Jewish Quarter of the city, which emptied out during WWII as people were killed or fled to other countries.[1]

The first such bar, Szimpla Kert, opened in 2002. These pubs often leave features exposed and walls unplastered, decorating with found furniture and objects. At first they were part of an alternative scene but have grown in popularity and size.

They have also had an impact on the neighborhoods that house them. Szimpla Kert declares that "the ruin pub is the post-modern culture cent[er]." It acts as a civic base and art incubator, and has worked to improve the neighborhood around its location to make it more pedestrian-friendly.

These unique buildings proved to be a perfect home for Gyurkovics's games. The company name, ParaPark, intentionally plays on the "para-normal" to suggest a certain strangeness or edginess to the games.

And the games are continuing to evolve along with the city. Rising rent prices are making it hard to find cheap real estate in the city center, and there's demand for activities for larger groups.

Luckily, the city is full of amazing parks, buildings, and monuments. New ParaPark adventures will send people out into the streets, allowing them to move at their own pace through the sights and textures of Budapest, using puzzles to create a whole new playground to explore and enjoy.

SCRAP

Small groups of people clutch sheets of paper.

They wander around a room, staring at the walls, which are covered in letters and symbols. Nearby, a row of candy dispensers sits to the side.

The symbols on the wall seem to have some meaning, but it isn't obvious to the people, at least not yet. They're taking diligent notes, consulting with one another in whispers.

Someone spots a riddle on the ceiling.

"'A equals something that only exists in the day but gets longer in the evening,'" they read aloud.

One of the team members quickly gets the answer to the riddle: "A shadow."

The team fills in their answer sheet, hands it in to a game monitor, and receives a coin in return.

A player slots it into the candy machine and receives a plastic capsule filled with paper shapes.

They realize that arranging the shapes will start them on the next puzzle, so they get to work, excited to see where the trail will lead.

This is a scene from an early SCRAP game, circa 2009.

SCRAP was the first company to create in-person puzzle rooms inspired by the Crimson Room online escape game by Toshimitsu Takagi, after creating real-world games to coincide with an article written about their digital counterparts.

They were the first "formal" escape room company to open in the United States, establishing industry standards for game format, room layout, and puzzle structure.

———————

Takao Kato wanted to create adventures.

Since 2004, he had been publishing a free bimonthly magazine, *SCRAP*. Part of the magazine's business model was to organize paid ticketed events that were thematically related to the printed content. For example, if they wrote an article about board games, they would sell tickets to a meetup event where people could drink beer and play those board games for themselves.

Kato had a conversation with a friend who was obsessed with online escape games like Crimson Room and published an article about it in the magazine. At the time, he had no idea that it would spawn a puzzling empire.

"These days, I'm often asked, 'How did you come up with the idea of the REAL ESCAPE GAME?'" Kato wrote on the Real Escape Game website. "I can't say anything really cool. I just answer like this: 'I was thinking about doing some kind of new event, and the girl sitting next to me said she was hooked on online escape games, so I just tried to make one.'"

This modest answer reveals little about the puzzling empire that SCRAP would evolve to encompass, and the worlds of adventure that they hope to evoke.

"Our philosophy is to create things in our daily lives that we have only seen in the world of stories," he wrote on the Real Escape Game website.

"For example, a bomb will explode in 10 seconds. I have scissors in my hand. And you have to cut either the blue or red wire. I think you've seen such a scene dozens of times in dramas, manga, and movies. Our job is to actually bring it to life."

Their design approach comes from two objectives: first, to create an interesting, "impossible" setting or environment, and second, to actually make it real for people.

In 2007, after speaking to a friend who loved online Flash escape games like Crimson Room, *SCRAP* magazine published a story on the puzzle games and organized a "real escape game" as its corresponding ticketed event.

Their first event was in Kyoto, Japan, and despite being advertised only through a small ad in the paper, all 150 tickets were sold.

Their next event, held in Osaka, also sold out, and Kato knew that they were onto something special. Players were excited by the opportunity to work as a team toward shared goals, and to feel a sense of accomplishment they weren't finding in other parts of their lives.

When SCRAP was first starting out, Kato told Edan Corkill of the *Japan Times* that they had to push hard against stereotypes of gamers as being nerds with no social skills, and to elevate the idea of gaming as a worthy pastime.[2]

"Anything that blurs the line between reality and fantasy tends to be perceived negatively in Japan these days," he said, but added that "stories have the power to make the real world a better place."

In a 2009 interview, Kato described being jealous of characters in books and comics. "I wondered why interesting things didn't happen in my life, like they did in books," he said. "I thought I could create my own adventure, a story, and then invite people to be a part of it."

SCRAP saw an opportunity for using empty buildings and unused spaces to set the stage for their games. By hosting events in bars and classrooms after hours, the company was able to run games without the overhead of paying rent, and the venues lent a surreality to the games' atmosphere that players seemed to enjoy.

"In a room in an empty building, or at a deserted amusement facility, if we bring a story and a puzzle, people will come," Kato said in a 2020 interview with Manabink's Ryoji Shimada.[3]

In 2010, they ran several events in amusement parks; one in Yomiuriland in Tokyo, and one in Nagashima Spa Land in Mie Prefecture. In 2011, the company rented a baseball stadium called the Tokyo Dome for three days, running two-hour events for 1,200 participants at a time, with twelve thousand visitors overall.

Over the next year, they expanded into Shanghai, Taiwan, Singapore, and San Francisco, opening permanent physical locations as well as running games in temporary or unused spaces.

The San Francisco venue was the first formal escape room venue in the United States, setting into motion a new industry of experiential gameplay.

"We live in a world where we can theoretically do anything we want," Kato wrote on the SCRAP site.[4]

"It is, however, so difficult to really feel free in our actions and really have fun with others. When people are trapped with people they don't know with challenges to solve, they are free to get really into it because they have control on the adventure.... The game was created so that anyone with good ideas, creativity, and good communication skills can manage to escape. But there aren't many places like this around us. This place creates a kind of energy that was needed, yet never created anywhere else. When confronted with time limits and confined spaces, people think outside of the box and really have a blast.

"I often think that the normal life we lead could become meaningful if we changed how we look at it," Kato concluded. "Imagine if there was a secret code underneath this desk, or if a key was hidden under the sofa, or if the young man next to you had a secret letter. If you look at the world as if it were an adventure like this, I think it would be kind of nice and mysterious. . . . The stories we encounter make our everyday lives better, and having a better everyday life will surely produce even better stories."

CHAPTER 10

The 2010s to Now: The Rise of Escape Room Games

I think that pretty much every form of fiction (I'd include fantasy, obviously) can actually be a real escape from places where you feel bad, and from bad places. It can be a safe place you go, like going on holiday, and it can be somewhere that, while you've escaped, actually teaches you things you need to know when you go back, that gives you knowledge and armour and tools to change the bad place you were in.

So no, they're not escapist. They're escape.

—NEIL GAIMAN

And now we reach our favorite topic, escape rooms!

We're in the midst of a wonderful movement of innovative, immersive work. With increasing numbers of digital puzzle games on the market, like 2012's The Room series, people have a vocabulary for understanding new creations, and artists are pushing boundaries as they explore new forms, themes, and methods of delivery for real-world games and creative experiences.

And while there are franchises, branded games, and large operations, escape rooms are still largely a DIY, small-business industry.

Escape rooms are also exploring new, exciting forms with in-person experiences, at-home tabletop games, virtual-only experiences run via video-conferencing software, podcasts that run audio-only games, and DIY games that people run for their friends.

FUN AND FRIENDSHIP

"Quickly!" someone shouts.

The group of people are hurriedly jamming colorful wires into ports on a plastic box with a red light, a switch, and a power plug.

They plug the box into a big, retro computer bank, the red light turns on, and they flip the switch.

Boom.

The room shakes with a deep rumble. The lights flicker on and off, finally cutting out completely.

Suddenly, a light turns on. On the ceiling, there's a number being projected: 1258.

"The door code!"

The group exits, triumphant.

They're greeted by a secretary, who less than one hour before was trying to stop them from entering the room.

They successfully bribed her with a set of ration coupons, but now she's come back from her lunch break and is ready to shoo them away before the officials come to investigate—whatever it was they did in there.

She smiles, breaking character. "Congratulations," she tells the group. "You escaped just in time!"

The group cheers, high-fiving one another. The tension of the timer is gone, the magic spell of being in the room is broken, and they have emerged on the other side, triumphant.

There's a brief pause before someone poses a question to the rest of the group.

"So when can we do another one?"

Escape rooms are a bona fide phenomenon, with thousands popping up in cities all around the world, but they're part of a long, continuing legacy of in-person entertainment, gameplay, puzzles, and experience design—with a pinch of mystery and adventure thrown in.

According to the website Room Escape Artist, at the end of 2014 there were twenty-two escape room companies in the United States. In the next two years, that number grew rapidly, reaching over 900 by 2016. In early 2021, there were 2,250.[1]

The early games were often very basic. I played many that just placed simple furniture in a room with scraps of paper and rudimentary props. Many puzzles involved finding a number and entering it into a padlock or safe. But despite the basic setup, they were very fun! As soon as I played my first one, I knew I'd be hooked forever.

Over the next decade, the games flourished, rooms drawing design inspiration from haunted houses, theme parks, immersive theater, and adventure games. Now sets can be elaborate, movie-quality productions, with complicated electronic props and special effects.

The contemporary scene of escape rooms around the globe is thriving, with venues in many cities and appearances in pop culture like television and films.

Many venues now offer digital versions of their in-person experiences, so they can be experienced from the comfort of your own home, with friends from around the world.

And immersive entertainment continues to push artistic boundaries in every medium.

A bowling alley–scale art installation in Santa Fe, New Mexico, called Meow Wolf introduces visitors to a seemingly normal family home. Upon closer inspection, however, every closet, fireplace, and household appliance is a portal to a different surreal, sci-fi environment. The space is half theme park, half artist showcase.

In virtual reality, companies like Tender Claws are combining digital environments with live performance, creating spaces and stories about people, places, and the nature of time that can be explored in ways that would not be possible in the physical world.

And in Los Angeles, California, environmental artists are designing spaces that tell touching stories. In Jeff Leinenveber and Jarrett Lantz's the Nest, visitors move through an intimate space, a storage unit left behind after the death of a woman named Josie. By listening to cassette tapes and exploring her belongings, they come to understand the arc of this woman's life.

A group called Odyssey Works explores the concept of performance by inverting it: instead of a large group of people watching a show in front of them, their performances focus on an audience of one. The experiences are personal and meaningful, woven into the person's life, and can last days, weeks, or months. They are an expression of the power of seeing and being seen, and of how an experience can be a gift that we give to another person.

It is an exciting world of art and experiences that informs the design of contemporary escape rooms. The longer they're around, the more the tech, design, theater, puzzles, set design, and gameplay will evolve.

What will the future hold for this industry as technology evolves, creative skills improve, new formats appear, and customers get more savvy? It's fun to imagine and impossible to predict. However it turns out, I'll be first in line to buy a ticket. I hope I'll see you there.

You've learned everything about how we got to escape rooms, what drives their creation, and what makes them so popular.

Next, let's teach you how to play them yourself.

PART 2

AN ESCAPE ROOM TOOL KIT

Now you know how we got here, a journey that took us from the ancient Indus Valley to our phones, pocket-size computers more powerful than the machines that took the first spacecraft to the moon.

What do you do, now that we've arrived?

You play!

———————

There are many types of escape rooms and puzzle games, and this guide will help you with each of them.

We'll discuss how to form a team and play well together, plus tips for success in any game (not just escape rooms). You'll also be able to tackle puzzle games with aplomb, since we'll talk about how clues work, and explore common codes, types of puzzles, and red herrings.

For in-person or virtual games, I'll walk you through what to look for when you get a peek at a room for the first time, and teach you what a game monitor is thinking while they're keeping an eye on you and giving hints.

For at-home games, we'll talk about how to pick a game, set up your space, recruit your friends and family, and avoid spoilers.

And lots more.

Once you start to build your puzzle skill set, you'll find many avenues to apply them, and ways to enjoy them. (I'll recommend a few of these paths, too.)

Puzzles have existed forever, of course, but I really think that we're in a wonderful age where there are plenty of new games, in every medium imaginable, for us to enjoy.

So, let's dig deep into the world of playing escape rooms. There's a lot to learn, and it's going to be a lot of fun.

Onward!

CHAPTER 11

Types of Rooms

So you want to play an escape room game. Great!

Maybe you've driven by one, or seen one featured in a television show or on the news. Maybe you have a friend who's super into them, and you're curious about trying them out. Or maybe someone just thought you'd like this book because you're into games.

Whatever the case: welcome!

When it comes to escape rooms and puzzles, there are *so* many options to choose from: an in-person game, a virtually hosted game, a video game, a board game, even a book.

The world, as they say, is your oyster.

IN-PERSON GAMES

In-person escape room games are probably the most familiar to you. These are team-based games set in physical spaces that are highly decorated. Everything in the room is a puzzle to solve or a clue to discover. Usually you have a timer, often (but not always!) set to one hour.

For these games, you'll go to a company's location and check in before being led into the game room.

VIRTUAL AND AVATAR GAMES

There are two types of escape rooms that can be played online, an avatar game and a digital, or virtual, escape room. Often, both of these will have a physical host on a video call with you.

Because these are sometimes based in real, physical game rooms that existed before being converted to run as digital games, these companies often run in-person, ticketed sessions, too. Be sure to double-check the listing to make sure you're booking the online version of the game.

In an avatar game, you'll join the game using video-conferencing software or log in to the company's website. You will have a first-person point of view, as your avatar stands in a physical escape room.

In this type of game, you and your team can direct the avatar, just like a character in a video game, asking them to pick things up, explore the room, examine objects, and enter solutions to puzzles. They may speak with you, or they may just gesture.

In an avatar game, you will likely be given digital versions of the objects in the room as you find them, so you can examine them more closely. This will be part of your "inventory," or the list of items you collect as you play.

These inventory items might be sent to you as photographs or computer files, or you might have to open a shared folder to access them. You may also be sent videos to look at online, or other websites to look for information or do an interaction.

For this reason, it's helpful to play on a computer rather than a tablet, so that you can look at the files and still keep an eye on the game.

In the other kind of virtual game, you may play a session with or without a host. For these games, you'll join using video-conferencing software, or log in to the company's website.

These types of games are likely to have been designed specifically for online play, rather than as an adaptation of a physical game. So sometimes they'll be self-directed, without the need for a host.

If the game has no host, it is likely available "on demand." That means that you can buy a ticket and play it immediately, rather than needing to book a specific timed session. So if you're looking for something to do right away, this is a great option!

If there is a host, they will speak to you and guide you through the game's websites, files, or other types of gameplay. They may also be "in character," acting out scenes or performing dialogue. Some puzzles may require you to interact with them, giving you instructions or asking questions.

But mostly, you will drive yourself through the game, solving puzzles and entering codes to progress.

Both of these types of digital games are a lot of fun, and a lot of them are brand new. If you have friends or family who live in other cities, it's a great way to spend quality time together. It's also a fun way to experience rooms far away, even in other countries, when traveling isn't an option.

Be sure to check out the game's technology requirements beforehand, and give yourself enough time before the game starts to get set up and connected properly. It's no fun to look forward to a game only to find out that you can't hear the host's voice because of some obscure setting in your Internet browser.

VIDEO GAMES

There are lots of wonderful escape room and puzzle video games available online, from phone app stores, for download on a computer, and to play on a virtual-reality headset. Some are timed, some are not.

Some of my favorites:

The Room (series) by Fireproof Games (2012)

The Room is an excellent series of games and can be found in most phone app stores. Each game starts with a mysterious, locked puzzle box. The player fiddles with the box's mechanical locks, figuring out how to solve each one.

This is a great way to get a feel for how sequential games work, with one solution opening up the next puzzle, and so on. There are also several sequels to the original, so if you're a fan of this style of game, there's a lot of fun to be had. Their virtual-reality sequel, The Room VR: A Dark Matter, is especially fun.

I Expect You to Die by Schell Games (2016)

I Expect You to Die is a virtual-reality game. The player is a James Bond–like secret agent, and like Bond, they must get out of a series of tricky, slightly absurd situations. In this game, you start out stuck inside a gadget car, inside a cargo plane. Can you avoid a deadly laser retina scan, or cut the right wire on a bomb so that you can drive the car out of the plane to safety?

Tick Tock: A Tale for Two by Other Tales Interactive (2019)

Tick Tock: A Tale for Two is a wonderful game with intriguing illustrations. It requires two computers or screens to play. It can be played with someone in person, as long as you can't see each other's screens, or even over the phone or on a video call.

In this game, each player is shown a unique screen that contains information the other player will need to use. You have to communicate about what you're seeing and what information you're given, so that you can both complete a series of puzzles.

BOARD GAMES

If you're a tabletop game fan, you're in luck! There are tons of escape room board games available. Board games and other tabletop-based play are a great way to spend time with friends and family in a setting without screens.

Escape Room in a Box: The Werewolf Experiment (Mattel)
2–6 players

In one hour, players use the components in this board game box to solve a series of puzzles to create an antidote that will stop them from transforming into werewolves.

You do use up some of the components during gameplay, but it is possible to purchase replacement parts so that you can pass the game along, or even run it for other people.

Box One Presented by Neil Patrick Harris (Theory11)
1 player

Box One is a board game for one person at a time. Harris has an interest in magic (as in, sleight of hand, cards, and illusions) and that influence is definitely present in this whimsical game.

Although it's a game designed for one person, I think that a teen and a parent or a couple might enjoy playing it together. But if you choose to play alone, the game is resettable and no components are used up in gameplay, so you can share it with friends and family when you're done.

My spoiler-free tip: in escape rooms and other puzzle games, it's normal to disassemble everything, examine it all carefully, and then figure out what to use now versus later. In this game, that will spoil some really wonderful moments of surprise, so leave everything in place until the game directs you to touch something. I promise, it's worth the wait.

Sherlock Holmes: Consulting Detective (various publishers)
1+ players

This isn't strictly a puzzle game, but I include it because it touches on many of the things that make escape rooms fun: it has a high level of immersion, it uses paper ephemera for storytelling, and it works the brain.

Consulting Detective presents a series of mysteries set in Victorian London, told through casebooks. The players are Sherlock Holmes's assistants. He's already figured out the solutions, of course, but he wants to test your mettle and has challenged you to work your way through maps, newspapers, address books, and paper-based conversations to investigate what you think happened and solve the case.

If you like deduction games and mystery stories, you'll likely enjoy this. Some of the cases can be tricky, but the experience of trying to solve things and reading out the dialogue outweighs the potential ups and downs of the individual mysteries.

It was first published in the 1980s, and there have been several additional sets of cases published since then, so there's plenty of content to enjoy.

TABLETOP PUZZLE GAMES

These are similar to board games but are presented in a different way. Maybe it's a set of paper printouts; maybe it's a subscription box that comes in the mail, surprising you with a new mystery every week.

Dr. Esker's Notebook by Plankton Games

This game is a deck of illustrated cards containing a series of fun puzzles to solve. The puzzles are slightly more advanced, but it's a game that can be put away and returned to, making it easy to take some time to think about the puzzles. Pen and paper recommended.

Puzzled Pint by various authors

Puzzled Pint is a monthly puzzle-solving event that started in Portland, Oregon. Every month, its organizers post a "location puzzle" that when solved reveals the name of a local bar, restaurant, or online hangout where puzzle solvers will congregate on the second Tuesday.

There, players receive a packet of puzzles and spend several pleasant hours hanging out and making solves.

Every month since 2010, the Puzzled Pint creators have released a free set of medium-difficulty puzzles for people to solve. You can look into their vast archive and pick a set from the many fun, geeky themes, and print them out to solve at home.

You can also join an in-person or digital meetup every second Tuesday of each month.

Visit http://puzzledpint.com for more information and to find the printable puzzles.

Ravensburger Escape Puzzles

Ravensburger is a top-notch jigsaw puzzle company, so when I saw that they had made a series of "escape puzzles," I knew I had to try them out.

These function like an ordinary jigsaw puzzle, in that you assemble pieces on a flat surface. But immediately, you'll notice that there's something strange—the image on the pieces doesn't quite match the one on the box. The scenes are transformed, full of hidden clues to solve once the puzzle has been fully assembled.

BOOKS

Some of these puzzle books can be a little advanced, so they may be something you want to seek out a bit further down the road. They're also untimed, so you can play whenever you like.

Puzzlesnacks: More Than 100 Clever, Bite-Size Puzzles for Every Solver
        by Eric Berlin (2019)
http://puzzlesnacks.com

Good for all ages. More than one hundred puzzles of thirty-nine different types.

Journal 29: Interactive Book Game by Dimitris Chassapakis (2017)
http://journal29.com

This book has 148 pages with sixty-three puzzles and riddles to solve. Challenging puzzles. Answers are entered online, so Internet access is required.

The Maze of Games by Mike Selinker and Pete Venters (2014)
http://lonesharkgames.com

Fifty challenging puzzles and a story about two children lost in a world of mazes. Great for advanced players.

CHAPTER 12

Succeeding Before
You Even Start

In the previous part of this book, you learned about the *why* of escape rooms. Let's tackle the *what* and the *how*.

Finding an in-person escape room near you is simple. Your best bet is to go to your nearest search engine and type "escape rooms near me." If you've never played one before, don't worry about picking the very best one—you're there to learn, and even simple rooms are great practice. Most rooms will list their difficulty levels from easy to expert, or using a number rating, such as 1/5 to indicate the simplest game or 5/5 for the most difficult.

Go ahead and try a beginner or intermediate room first. It may be too simple, it may be too hard . . . but then you'll know, which will help you make a choice next time. As we'll shortly discuss, losing and learning from mistakes, and trying again and again, is a big theme in escape rooms, and one of the things that keeps people coming back.

If you can't find a time and date that work for you, try emailing or calling the company directly. Sometimes companies are willing to do a show earlier or later than other shows on their schedule, or during a weekday, for an additional fee.

Also, many companies don't put pictures of their rooms on their websites, to try to preserve the element of surprise. As a customer, I find I prefer sites that do include them. But if there are no pictures, take a look at the themes on offer. Do you like the genre of movie that a room is themed after? Is the story line intriguing? You can also always call up a company to ask for more details and ask for recommendations.

You can also search the Internet for spoiler-free reviews. Reviewers for escape-room-enthusiast sites often travel, so they may have played a game in your area and will have good insight into what a room's strengths and weaknesses might be—without ruining the fun.

Or ask around! Your friends or people in your network might have played a game near you and can give you tips on whether you'll enjoy it. Maybe they'll even be interested in joining your team for a new play session.

Speaking of teams, that's the next step for a new player: you'll need to put a group together. It could be members of your family, people you play board games with, coworkers, someone you want to take on a date, or even total strangers. (The next chapter covers team-forming strategies in more detail.) In all these cases, the following tips will be especially important.

That's because an escape room is a kind of crucible: it's a high-pressure environment, and you really get to see people's true personalities emerge.

Hence, my number one tip for escape room success: **communication**. Escape rooms are all about finding information, sharing what you've found, and using it creatively. So if everyone's finding information, but nobody's sharing it, you're going to be in trouble.

Number two: **have a game plan**. You're reading this book, so you've probably guessed by now that there are specific strategies for tackling an escape room. We'll discuss several.

Number three: **watch the clock**. Ultimately, you're playing for fun.

But beating the clock is the way to win. Keeping an eye on the time, using hints, and asking for help when you get stuck will be key.

Number four: **do your research**. Study the information laid out in this book (learn how codes work, examine padlocks, etc.) and you'll be well prepared to succeed in a game.

Number five: **eyes on the prize**. The goal of escape rooms is, well, to escape. Or to save the day, find the magical object, defuse the bomb, and so on. Every step of the game is driving you toward this end goal, so don't get distracted by misleading objects or puzzles that don't actually need solving. (We'll talk about this in detail soon.) If you need a hint to move toward this end goal, take it.

Number six: **have fun**. Yes, it's a challenge; it's team building; it's a detailed story world. But it's also a game, and you're there to enjoy it. Be nice to your teammates, the game monitor, and yourself.

Armed with this book, you're sure to have a great time.

CHAPTER 13

Putting a Team Together

Your team is a vital part of your escape room experience. No room can be solved by just one person, so you're going to have to trust and rely on one another to get through it and make it out as winners.

When you're just starting out, unless you play a lot of other types of games together already, you're unlikely to know the strengths and weaknesses of your other team members—or your own. As you get better at playing rooms, you'll also learn to recognize what you're good at, and what's better left to someone else.

There are lots of ways to find potential teammates, though.

If your friends or family aren't interested, there are online communities for fans of escape rooms, so you might be able to find people there. Let them know that you're a new player, interested in playing for the first or second time. The community is very friendly, and you're sure to find someone who can give you tips and recommendations.

You can also try local message boards like Craigslist, Meetup, or Nextdoor. All of these have game-focused groups, so try posting there to see if anyone bites.

By the way, if you're booking an in-person game, note that most escape room companies don't allow young children, and some don't allow young teenagers. This could be for legal reasons, or because they won't enjoy the puzzles, or because the theme is too mature. Make sure you check the rules on the company's website.

If you're playing a video game or board game version of an escape room and want to include kids, keep an eye on them to see if they're becoming bored or frustrated. They may need a little extra hand to keep them engaged.

CHAPTER 14

What to Know Before You Go

Okay, so you've found an escape room that looks fun and booked tickets, or bought the game to play at home or on your computer. Fantastic!

What next?

The following chapters break down various types of games and how to approach them. But whichever you choose, there are a few universal rules that will set you up for success in any game-playing situation.

First, talk to your team about expectations. Here are some questions to discuss:

WHAT IS OUR STRATEGY FOR SOLVING THE ROOM?

Are you going to barge into a game room and tear everything apart, or are you going to set up a grid method like an archaeologist? (I'm mostly joking about that one, but hey, whatever works for you.) For digital games, are you going to use the in-game chat room, or set one up yourself on a private server or group chat?

It's good to know these things in advance so that everyone in your group is on the same page and so you have time to troubleshoot if there are any technology snafus.

HOW WILL WE COMMUNICATE INFORMATION?

When games are ongoing, it's easy to get wrapped up in what you're doing and ignore everyone else. The problem is, you might have found something that a person on the other side of the room needs, or vice versa, or spotted something in the corner of a screen or inside a digital folder.

Unless you talk about it, you're never going to solve any puzzles. So always call out when you find something new, and pay attention when others speak up.

It's also helpful to have someone be an unofficial timekeeper. Sometimes a game will include an automated countdown timer, sometimes not. Time flies when you're having fun, so I like to watch the clock and keep an eye on our progress. Plus, it's a good way to know if you're spending too long on an individual puzzle.

And that leads to . . .

WILL WE ASK FOR HINTS?

Okay, personally, I think you should always, always ask for hints. So maybe the question should be "*When* will we ask for hints?"

If I've spent more than five minutes trying to get a puzzle, and there's no obvious way forward, I'll pull in another teammate. If there's no progress after, say, two minutes, I'll ask for a hint. I like to keep the game moving, because it's more fun that way (and, I believe, you're more likely to win). And because games generally aren't replayable, I like to see the ending.

But be aware that to some people, asking for a hint feels like admitting defeat.

Not knowing how to solve something isn't a failure. It takes a lot of guts to be able to raise your hand and ask for help.

And anyway, most hints will just be subtle nudges to get you on the right track. Nine times out of ten, a player is actually pretty close to the solution, and their thought process just needs a little tweaking. The one remaining time, they're waaaay off, so the hint is even more important, to stop them from wasting any more time.

WILL WE TRY TO COMPLETE EVERY PUZZLE, OR WILL WE MOVE ON ONCE THE LARGER PUZZLE IS SOLVED?

This one comes up frequently with advanced puzzle solvers.

Sometimes, you can solve a puzzle—by this, I mean you can get the code or info out of it that you need to move on—but the larger framework of the puzzle has more to complete.

For example, let's say you're presented with a big crossword grid. You only need to solve five of the words to fill in a set of circled letters, which is the code that you need to move on. But there are still twenty-five more words on the grid.

Obviously, in that case, you should put the crossword down when you've gotten the code and move on to whatever's next.

But in the heat of the moment, that isn't always clear to people. It can feel weird and uncomfortable to leave something unfinished. The urge to complete a puzzle is a powerful one!

Here's another extremely common scenario: you've got a padlock, and it's the only thing standing between you and the next section of the game.

You solve the first three digits—let's say by finding a hidden number in a painting on the wall. There's a fourth painting, and you know it has the fourth digit in it . . . but you could also just spin the last wheel, trying all ten digits from 0 to 9, until it opens.

Will your team wait until the last digit has been solved through the puzzle, or is it okay to try spinning the dial so that you can move on quicker? Is the feeling of completion more fun, or the satisfaction of speed?

This may seem silly to ask about, but I assure you, emotions can run high when you find yourself in the moment. There's no right answer—it's down to personal preference, so chat about it with your group and see if you can come to an agreement in advance. And if you do encounter this scenario during the game, ask your friends if they mind before going ahead and doing it, even if you agreed ahead of time. It's only polite.

WILL WE KEEP SPOILERS TO OURSELVES IF WE SPOT SOMETHING?

As you get to be a more advanced player, you'll also want to talk about things like spoilers.

If you see a hidden door, is it okay to announce it to the rest of the group? (See chapter 24 about padlocks and other locking mechanisms for ways that doors can be concealed.) Or is it better to save the surprise for when it's revealed as part of the gameplay?

As you learn more about puzzles and codes, you'll start to spot more quickly the ways information is hidden.

With an advanced puzzle-solving team, it's probably no big deal to call stuff out as you see it, because it saves time.

But with a new team, a lot of the joy of playing comes from the surprise of realizing something is hidden and seeing what it is revealed to be.

So shouting out what it is before another player realizes it can deflate the vibe. Assess the relative game-playing level of your team and see if you can work it out beforehand.

WHAT SHOULD WE DO IF TEMPERS ARE RUNNING HIGH?

Maybe your group of friends is the most laid-back set of people in the world—if so, that's wonderful!

I still find that it's helpful if everyone agrees to try to have fun and be nice to one another.

That means, if you feel yourself getting too stressed out or frustrated, you'll remember to step back, take a deep breath, and calm yourself down. (And also to graciously accept the advice to do so, if someone else suggests it.)

And also? *Take hints.* Seriously, if something is confounding you to the point where you're losing your temper, you've moved beyond the realm of having fun. Do what you must to always bring things back to fun.

———————

You can return to this set of questions regularly as you become a more advanced player or find different groups. As you'll learn, regardless of level, strong communication and regularly checking in with your teammates will continue to serve you throughout your gameplay.

CHAPTER 15

Which Type of Escape Room Player Are You?

I've watched thousands of game sessions, and after a while, you start to notice some distinct player patterns.

THE EXPLORER

This person searches the entire room, probing every corner and touching every object to discover its secrets. If there's something hidden, they're the one most likely to discover it.

Need to know: If people think the room has been searched completely by someone else, they're less likely to double-check to make sure that's actually true. If the explorer missed something the first time around, it could go unfound until another player has a look around for themselves.

THE CODEBREAKER

This person is On. The. Case. If a puzzle is found, they're right there to solve it. They know all the codes and methods and they're eager to get their hands on everything. Sharing the work with other people is a balancing act, but if they're doing it right, everyone will have a lot of fun, together.

Need to know: If you're working on a puzzle for a while and not making any progress, grab a teammate and hand it off to them. Sometimes having a fresh set of eyes on it is all it takes to solve it.

THE WATCHER

This person steps back and sees what's happening in the whole room. They can be the person checking in with everyone, asking, "Who's working on what? Has this item been used yet? How did this lock get opened?" This person is a strategist, helping make connections that people working up close might not have noticed. They may be able to see that a puzzle would be great for someone's special skills and put it into their hands so it gets solved quickly.

Need to know: It's fine for multiple people to switch from being deeply engrossed in puzzles to stepping back and observing the bigger picture. Not everyone has to be performing 100 percent of the time, and it helps keep the overall view fresh if several people are monitoring progress.

THE CHEERLEADER

This person may not be the biggest fan of escape rooms, but they sure are a huge fan of the team. This person might wander between puzzles, not solving anything themselves, but offering support, feedback, and insight to people who are working on a puzzle.

Need to know: There's a fine line between supporting and distracting, and attempting and ignoring. Even if you feel like you aren't contributing, give a puzzle a try—you might be surprised!

There are also some less positive archetypes that I've seen. I'll outline them now, along with some tips for how to gently redirect these behaviors.

THE DIRECTOR

This person is the boss, and they and everyone else in the room know it. (Sometimes, as in a team-building exercise for work, it's the group's literal boss.)

This person lays down the law, making declarations about how something works, what the code should be, who should be doing what. Everyone else obeys, afraid to contradict the director's mandates.

The problem is, escape rooms are a team sport. If the director is wrong, the whole team loses out on a chance to work toward victory.

Sometimes this can't be avoided, so talk to your team beforehand, and make a plan to amplify one another's voices. If you hear someone say an answer that gets ignored, echo it: "Francisco had a good idea, let's try that one." Phrase it as a statement instead of asking permission to try things— or better yet, just get in there (politely) and enter the solve yourself.

THE HOARDER

This person is the dark side of the explorer. They love to find stuff, but they don't tell anyone else they've found it. They may quietly go and enter a code into a padlock, unlocking a box and revealing a whole new set of clues. But if nobody else knows it's happening, it's no good for the team.

Having a watcher on the team can be a good way to nip this in the bud: if someone is checking in with various team members to see what they're working on and what's been solved, they can be the ones to shout it out to the rest of the team so that solving can continue.

THE HOGGER

This person is the dark side of the codebreaker. They want to be the one who solves every puzzle, enters every code, finds every hidden thing. They may even snatch puzzles or items out of someone's hand in their excitement. Or they may be totally stuck on a puzzle and unwilling to stop working on it, even when all possible attempts have been made.

This is a great place for a teammate to step in and either offer alternative methods for solving, suggest another player try it out, or, most likely, flag the need for a hint from the game monitor.

THE NAYSAYER

Escape rooms can be frustrating, but that's part of the fun. Unfortunately, the naysayer doesn't hesitate to let you know exactly how frustrated they are. This has the consequence of dragging the rest of the team's mood down, because who wants their teammate to be unhappy?

Give the naysayer a specific role or ask for their help. Is there a puzzle that still needs solving, or an answer that should be double-checked?

This can help them keep their focus on the game instead of on their complaints. They may make an excellent watcher, someone who can keep an eye on everything that's going on and make connections between puzzles.

Are you the naysayer? Try to turn yourself into the cheerleader or the watcher. Instead of complaining or critiquing, use the famous technique from improv: always answer, "Yes, and . . ."

· This could be pointing out that something has been attempted before, which isn't helpful on its own. But if you can offer a new option, it may just be the thing that cracks the case.

You can ask if there's something that hasn't been solved yet, or what information hasn't been used. Searching the room again can reveal something that was overlooked the first time.

Feeling too frustrated? Take a breather. Not every single member has to be solving 100 percent of the time. If you need to sit down and stare at the wall for a minute to clear your head, do it before jumping back into the game.

Your team will thank you.

THE CHAOS AGENT

This person means well, but there are still some issues. They may be really excited, or have less experience with games and puzzles generally. They shout out options and solutions without thinking them through or considering how they might connect to other parts of the game.

In a team scenario, that can get confusing or distracting, especially if someone needs to take time out of their own game-playing to manage them.

Help the chaos agent rein it in by giving them a specific task to focus on—they're a perfect candidate to double-check a search of the room, or to dig through a pile of books to see if any clues are hidden inside them.

Be sure to notice when team members get a solve or make a connection, and congratulate them out loud. Maybe add in a high five if you're feeling really great about it. Escape rooms move fast, so it can be nice to make the effort to point that out in the moment.

PRO TIPS FROM ESCAPE ROOM REVIEWERS

Room Escape Artist is an amazing escape room review site. Cofounders Lisa and David Spira, with a growing team of reviewers, have been reporting on rooms, advocating for player safety, and cultivating community since 2014.

I spoke to them to ask for their best advice for new players and tips for tackling games.

What would you say to a first-time player?

David: There's a couple of things we tell people. First, this is not a test of intellectual ability. It's not something that you can use to prove whether you are smart. In fact, approaching it that way is detrimental because what this really is, is a teamwork and communication and observation challenge. And if you can approach it from that standpoint and check your ego at the door, then you're going to be successful.

Lisa: The next thing is that you have to embrace it. You have to go in wanting to do it. You're not going to have a good time if you're not ready to embrace that you might have a good time, or you're too cool for it.

Are there any tips you've learned from playing so many games?

David: One hard rule that we have is, for the time that we're in the game, your pockets do not exist. We've actually lost a game because someone found something and they were like, *Oh, this is probably important*. And then they put it in their pocket. It was the worst way to lose!

Lisa: We always encourage people if you're an introvert to speak up and if you're an extrovert to shut up.

How long should a player be spending on a single puzzle?

Lisa: We encourage people to not spend too long on anything. It's going to click for someone, if it doesn't click for you. That's okay! Just pass it off to someone with all of the things that you've noticed. Hand it along and find something new, because it will speak to someone. A well-designed game is going to have challenges that speak to different types of solving.

David: You know, if you are working on something for more than five minutes and you're not making any progress, it either means you don't have all the components or it means that you are not the person to solve it. Either way, hand it off.

What should new players be aware of when they first start playing a room?

Lisa: Call out what you see to help your team recognize what's in there. It might feel weird to be like, "I'm holding a red thing!" But someone else might be holding a red thing, and those red things might go together. What you're really looking for is pattern matching, things that might go with other things.

David: We often will, like, say, especially if we're stuck, like, call out anything that seems weird. A hole in the bottom of a drawer might be important.

Lisa: Or a statue with a weirdly square base.

Do you have tips for more experienced players who are playing with newbies?

David: We try to maintain the mystery. We'll do things like not explaining RFID (radio-frequency identification), not pointing out, "Hey, that bookcase is almost certainly a trapdoor."

Lisa: We realized at one point that it was fun going in with our friends, saying, "That's going to be a trapdoor!" and everybody in the room nods. But if we had brought a new player, we would have completely spoiled the best moment for them.

David: To a lesser extent, that also extends to when we're talking about the game after the fact. As reviewers, we ask people their favorite part and their least favorite part. But we do it in reverse order of how much experience each player has. When we're playing with someone who's brand-new, they can share their amazing moments. They might find out shortly after, depending upon who our teammates are, that the moment was very poorly done and should never have been like that. But the new player is still experiencing excitement from that.

Do you always talk about the game afterward?

David: I think it's really important to talk about the games after the fact. I think that's actually an essential part of the experience. It was in some ways more essential in the olden days, because there would be twenty puzzles that a team of ten had to split up and solve, and maybe if you were good you saw a quarter of the game.

You look back at the triumphs that your teammates had. Part of being a good experienced teammate is trying to be really aware of who does what, because inevitably, newbies will sometimes feel down about themselves. We try to make sure that they have their moments, that there's a thing they solve, so when we walk out and they're like, "I didn't do anything," you can say, "No, you solved that thing. And I saw you working on that other thing. That was great."

How do you pick which games to play?

Lisa: Many players will hear about a particular game or a particular company and go to their website. I would encourage new players to see if the company tells you which games are more approachable or better for newer players, to trust them. You're probably going to have more fun. And if they all seem to be equally appealing, pick the one with the theme you like.

How many players do you recommend for a team?

Lisa: Don't stuff the room. Even if they say you can bring ten people.

David: Yeah. Six people is about the maximum that I think can function properly. Every person you introduce after that, I think entropy starts to increase exponentially, and eventually, just like in real life, you end up needing project managers in your escape room to actually keep on top of what's going on.

Any tips for how to dress?

Lisa: You can wear totally normal clothes, but you probably don't want to wear heels or a skirt or a dress.

David: If you're going into a horror game, be aware that infrared cameras, which are frequently used, make leggings appear transparent in the dark.

How do you play games with a variety of levels of life experience?

David: New teams, especially new teams of highly educated people, often overestimate their skills.

Lisa: And underestimate their preteens.

CHAPTER 16

Taking Care of Your Body

Whether you're playing a game on-site or through a video call, at home at a tabletop or holding a tablet, you must remember that puzzle-solving is a mentally and physically taxing activity. Here are some tips for taking care of yourself, which will ensure you have a great experience and are able to perform at your maximum and successfully complete these games.

MAKE SURE YOU'VE EATEN FOOD AND HAD SOME WATER

Chess grandmasters, the most advanced players in the game of chess, train both their bodies and their minds in preparation for a tournament. That's because intense thinking is, in fact, extremely physically demanding.

The brain uses half the body's energy resources, even though it's only 2 percent of a person's body weight. And in stressful situations, breathing rates increase, blood pressure elevates, and muscles contract. The stress on the body in a master-level chess tournament is comparable to the experience of top athletes.

Okay, I'm not claiming that going into an escape room is like a multi-day chess tournament with some of the best players in the world. But it is a *lot* of sustained thinking, and it's always a good idea to take care of yourself.

So if you're booking a game session right before a regular mealtime, have a snack first so that you don't get hangry (hungry and angry) and take it out on your teammates.

Be sure to drink lots of water, too. You're going to be talking a lot during the game.

WEAR COMFORTABLE CLOTHES

You're going to be standing or sitting for an hour, so you should try to dress in clothes that will be comfortable for that amount of time. If you're visiting an in-person room, you *definitely* need comfortable shoes with plenty of support.

In an in-person game, you might also be moving around a lot: reaching, climbing, kneeling down. So pick clothes you can move around in. (Also, if you can, please wear pants that don't reveal your derriere when you're crouching down. The things I have seen . . .)

Time seems to stand still when you get really engrossed in a game, so it's easy to forget the stresses on the body.

It's only afterward, when you're reaching for something across a table and you feel how sore your back is, that you realize, "Oh, I was standing all that time without a break."

CHEW GUM

This one is a little tricky. Most in-person escape rooms probably won't allow you to chew gum in their games. Because if you drop it or spit it out, it's going to get ground into the carpet, or someone's going to touch it by accident when they're searching for clues. (Gross!)

But there are a lot of studies that show chewing gum can improve attention and cognitive performance, and even reduce stress—all stuff that you want during a complicated puzzle game.

So if you're attending an in-person game, keep that gum in your pocket. But if you're playing a virtual or tabletop game, feel free to unwrap it and get chewing.

CHECK IN WITH YOURSELF AFTER THE GAME

When you've finished playing, you might feel a dip in energy, since you've just spent the last hour or so in a high-pressure situation.

Give yourself some time to sit calmly and process what you've just gone through. If you've just played with friends, this is a great time to chat about the game, discuss what you liked doing, and celebrate fun moments and great solves from your teammates. (This is actually an important cognitive step—check out the next chapter on team building and cohesion for more.)

Do some stretching, eat a small snack, and drink some more water.

And then give yourself a high five for a job well done.

CHAPTER 17

Team Building and Cohesion

When you play an escape room, you're usually going into the experience as a team. It's always a good idea to hype up your team beforehand and get everyone excited for a fun time—and the techniques are backed up by science.

Jessica Outlaw, a researcher at behavioral science research firm The Extended Mind, shared with me some recommendations for team cohesion, based in cognitive science.

"Cultures form anytime a group of people gather," she said. "To make a team feel unified, create new symbols for your group that have meaning.

"Everything from the world of sports, things that fans and players do, are so good for getting a group of people to feel like a team," she said. "Setting these things up in advance will prime your team for a good group performance."

Here are some of her tips for creating a group identity.

COME UP WITH A TEAM NAME

If you love puns, you're in luck. A lot of games will require you to come up with a team name, but even for the ones that don't, it's fun to choose what you'll call yourselves, and it will make you feel more unified.

MAKE T-SHIRTS FOR YOUR GROUP, OR WEAR COSTUMES

Visuals are very important for group unity. "Having a T-shirt signals belonging to that group," Jessica says. If you get a team T-shirt, it's a visual indicator that you're all in it together, and afterward, it will be an artifact with the positive memories of the experience. Every time you put it on, you'll become a part of that team again.

If you're playing a digital game, make a plan for everyone to wear costumes that match the room's theme. Most games will offer to take a group "photo" via screenshot, so you'll have a chance to pose together and create a little souvenir.

HAVE AN INSIDE JOKE OR SECRET WORD

"Language is the foundation of culture and community," Jessica says. "Create slang, or a unique greeting to fit your group's needs."

CREATE A PHYSICAL SYNCHRONIZATION

"Rituals help us mark transitions in our lives," Jessica notes. Her suggestion: when everyone walks into the room, tap the top of the doorway. (If you've ever watched the television shows *Friday Night Lights* or *Ted Lasso*, about an American football team and a British football team, respectively, you'll see a motivational sign on the locker room wall that all the players touch as they pass.)

DANCE TOGETHER

"Do the Macarena, feel your bodies, see your teammates with your eyes," she says. "Get your minds going—it's like doing a wave at a sports game. You're forming one unit, working in sync."

EVERYONE LIKES PRESENTS

Get a small gift for everyone on your team. Something small, like Chap-Stick or a piece of candy. It's a small gesture, but people love gifts, and it helps make everyone feel like a unit.

TELL STORIES AFTER YOU'RE DONE

After you've completed the room, whether you've won or not, talk about it with your team. Go through it step by step, making sure to focus on who accomplished what, and celebrate your successes.

In larp, this process is called "froth." It's a collective mythmaking, gathering together to celebrate your achievements and those of your teammates, solidifying the shared narrative in your memory.

CHAPTER 18

Safety in Escape Rooms

O kay, before we get into how to play, we have to talk about what *not* to do in an escape room. Yes, we're going to talk about safety.

When you go to a physical escape room, one of the first things that happens is a safety briefing. It's a lot like being on an airplane, hearing the flight attendants talk about the location of life vests and how to use oxygen masks. It's info you hope you never have to use, of course. But if that moment ever arrives, you'll be glad you listened.

Safety in escape rooms is my number one concern, both as a player and as a designer. So I have to consider everything that could possibly go wrong, from the smallest problem to the largest, and then make sure it doesn't happen. There are also a lot of rules and regulations that help make sure everything is built to the latest safety standards. (We'll talk about this in a bit.)

I'll do everything that I can to keep people from harm, but I also need people to exercise their common sense. Escape room creators and players are partners in safety.

When I'm a player coming into someone else's escape room, I assume that they're the same as me—concerned with player safety and held to the same standards by local rules and regulations. The thing is, I don't know for sure. So I have to rely on my own skills and awareness, just in case.

163

Here's what to look out for and ask about, and what you should avoid doing.

BEING LOCKED IN

One question we get a lot is: "Are escape rooms really locked?"

The answer is: sometimes, but not always.

The first generation of escape rooms usually locked people into their rooms, and players literally had to escape the room. (These games are known as "locked room" or "exit games" around the world, for this reason.) Often, the last step in the game was finding a key that unlocked the final door, allowing players to leave the game.

But as more and more games were designed, it became less common. After all, there are lots of ways to give people a satisfying ending, or confirm that they've won the game, that don't involve unlocking a door.

Still, it's something you might encounter, so let's talk about it.

First, there are rooms that release their final door with a keypad or electronic lock. These doors are held shut with electromagnets (we'll talk more about these in chapter 24).

Electromagnets are two-part magnets that turn "on," or become magnetic, when an electric current is run through them. When the current is shut off, the magnet opens.

In escape rooms where the exit door is held shut with an electromagnet, there will usually be an emergency release button, in case someone needs to trigger the exit early for any reason. This button should be big and easy to see. (If it isn't, ask!)

These doors should ideally open automatically when a fire alarm goes off in the building.

Next, there are rooms that release with a door handle key or dead bolt. In these, your last step is usually to find the key that opens the lock. For additional safety, these types of rooms sometimes have an extra key placed near the door for use in emergencies.

If you're uncomfortable, try requesting that the door remain unlocked during the game.

CUFFS AND OTHER RESTRAINTS

Sometimes rooms will handcuff players, tie them up, or otherwise restrain them. Room Escape Artist's David and Lisa Spira shared this advice on maintaining safety in these scenarios: "If they're handcuffing you or locking you up and not explaining how to free yourself in an emergency, demand your money back and leave," David said. "That's not an acceptable practice at this point."

"You should always be able to free yourself in an emergency situation, and you should always be able to free yourself in a not-quite-emergency situation," Lisa added. "If you don't feel well, you should be able to exit the game."

"The exception may be if there is an actor who can guide you to safety, who's with you at all times," David said. But he still recommends that patrons ensure their safety by communicating with the person running the game.

CLIMBING ON THINGS

I have been in escape rooms that required people to climb ladders and crawl through tunnels, so I'll include this safety warning here. When it comes to climbing, use common sense.

Do not climb on furniture. Do not climb on bookcases. Do not roll a chair over and stand on it to try to reach something high up.

If you do need to climb, the gameplay should make it obvious—for example, if there's a padlock dangling from the ceiling at the top of a ladder, there's a good chance you'll need to use the ladder to reach it.

ELECTRICITY AND WIRES

In escape rooms, where anything could be a puzzle or a clue, it feels like anything is fair game. After all, that light bulb could have a secret hidden paper inside it, couldn't it? Or this enticing wire might have a key attached to the end, right?

In all likelihood, no. Rooms are supposed to confound and challenge you, but they're not trying to kill you. Please do not touch outlets, plugs, or cables. (Especially don't reach into a wall to pull out a wire.) Unplugging something might turn off a lamp, but it also might disconnect an electronic prop that needs to stay on in order to function.

If the room contains this kind of thing, you will probably receive information about it in your game briefing, but just in case, you've been warned!

TAKE YOUR TIME

The ticking timer in an escape room adds a lot of pressure to the situation, so remember to pause sometimes, take a breath, and look around. There's no need to rush around or to run in a game, and you don't want to drop a prop or break a computer (or yourself).

YOUR SAFETY AND COMFORT
ARE THE MOST IMPORTANT THING

If you feel at all nervous, call up your escape room beforehand and ask them if they lock their rooms or what other safety measures they have in place. You can also ask about these things when you arrive on-site. I'm sure they'll be happy to help you out!

CHAPTER 19

Barriers to Accessibility

Accessibility in gaming is an important topic.

Many in-person and online games are designed for the cultural "default" of someone who is able-bodied. The assumption for many in-person games is also that players will be able to stand for a full hour, or bend low and reach high.

And the designer may not have taken into account that 5 to 10 percent of the population has color blindness, or that one in every ten people has some hearing loss.

Escape rooms aren't often inherently accessible, but I believe the standard is improving all the time. If you have any accessibility needs, don't hesitate to call the game and ask how they can accommodate you.

Here's a list of possible accessibility challenges in escape rooms. These are important to keep in mind, especially if you know that someone on your team will likely encounter them.

TINY PRINT

Lots of escape rooms will have puzzles that include tiny print. If you need reading glasses, don't forget to bring them along.

DARKNESS

A lot of escape rooms keep the lights pretty dim. This is great for atmosphere, not as good if you need to see well. Some rooms will allow you to carry your own flashlight if you ask beforehand.

COLOR BLINDNESS

If you have color blindness, ask if there are any puzzles in the game that will be affected. The game may have alternate versions of the puzzle, or someone may be able to describe the puzzle elements so that you can differentiate between the components.

AUDIO PUZZLES

For those with hearing loss, audio puzzles can be a challenge. Call ahead and ask whether they can provide the text of any narration. Or you can designate another member of your team to describe specific sounds to a player who may need it.

MOBILITY

As noted, standing for long periods of time, bending, reaching and climbing can all be challenging for many players.

Many rooms contain chairs, or will provide one for you if possible, so call and ask before your game.

Newer games are more likely to be wheelchair-accessible.

CHAPTER 20

In-Person Experiences

Sometimes a friend will ask me about my job. Game design can be complicated to explain, so I usually start by asking them if they've ever played an escape room before. If they say no, I ask why.

The answer, surprisingly often, is: "I'm interested in escape rooms, but I don't want to pay a lot of money for a ticket and then fail at it because I didn't know what I was doing."

That feeling of pressure to succeed is totally understandable. Escape rooms can seem pretty mysterious, and on top of that, most rooms try carefully to preserve their secrets so that players come in fresh and unspoiled. So new players don't always know what to expect, and that's intimidating. But I believe that most people will find escape rooms to be a fun challenge, even if they're nervous about it.

Here, I'll describe how I tackle an in-person escape room. In extreme detail. Everything that follows is an articulation of my thought process along the way.

Every room silently communicates many things, if you know what to look out for. Once you're able to recognize those elements, you'll know what to expect from them and can plan how to solve them. And while this is specifically about how to solve an in-person escape room, these principles will apply to any puzzle game, whether it's online or in real life.

With practice, you'll develop your own thought process, so don't worry too much about memorizing it from the material presented here. By following the general pattern, you'll be well on the way to a successfully solved room.

So, how do I play these games?

Examine, gather, assess, test. That's the formula for escape room success. (Hey, that kinda rhymes!)

Picture the game as a big, blank map. Your task as a player is to figure out what the boundaries of that map are. What is or isn't a puzzle? What are the rules of logic that govern this strange new space?

You're going to be faced with a lot of information, all at once. There's decor, doors, locks, props, furniture . . . walking into the room and feeling bombarded by this sudden rush of detail can be a little overwhelming.

So to start, you'll want to examine the room.

Ask yourself: What puzzles, objects, or clues are immediately available?

That means walking and looking around. Touch everything. (Gently!) Remember to look high and low. You might not know what's a puzzle or clue at first, so just pay attention as you take it all in.

As you go, ask yourself: What objects can I pick up and move? If something *doesn't* move, it might be part of a puzzle, so remember where these items are in the room.

(By the way, the website Room Escape Artist recommends "finger strength only" to judge whether something is movable. That means, if you can push, pull, or manipulate it with only the strength your fingers, it probably is supposed to move. The game is not trying to trick you, so if you find yourself grunting while trying to move an object, or are bracing yourself against a piece of furniture to give something a good hard yank, it's probably not supposed to shift. If you're really unsure about an item, ask your game monitor for clarification.)

For items that *can* move: collect everything, and put them all together, ideally on a central table or surface that everyone can stand around.

Once things are gathered, assess what you have. On the table, group things by similarities. Are there items in a set? Items like book pages, playing cards, tiles of the same size? Sometimes there will be symbols repeating over multiple objects. Those probably go together.

Remember to say these observations out loud to the other players, too, so that they know what you've found and what's going on. (See chapter 21 for communication strategies and more on how to speak with your team.)

This is also a great time for players to split up. One person can work on grouping objects or trying to figure out what's currently solvable, while someone else has a look around for more clues, or to see what the objects might connect to.

And it's a good idea to have multiple people doing the search, because one player might spot something that another player overlooked. In our day-to-day lives, someone double-checking work that we've just completed can be kind of annoying. In an escape room, it's a very useful habit, and one that must be learned.

Example: One player finds a drawer with a playing card in it. On the other side of the room, a player finds an empty card box. They might think this isn't a useful item—after all, it's just an empty box. But if they call it out, the first player might realize that the playing card goes inside it.

So, we're starting to see the parts of the map, but not how they're laid out or how they connect.

Which brings us to: what information is around the room? Are there posters, books, pieces of paper? Using the skills you'll learn in "How Hints Work" (chapter 22), "How to Solve Any Escape Room Puzzle" (chapter 23), and "Common Codes and Ciphers" (chapter 25), you'll be able to identify potential clues and patterns to be used later or with objects that you've found so far.

What looks like it has potential? Are there any places to enter information, such as a computer, a number pad? Are there padlocks that must be opened? Do they require a key, a number, or a word? Are there any locked doors, boxes, or cabinets?

One way to approach puzzle-solving is to identify its end point, then work backward.

There are lots of ways to conceal things (see chapter 24, "Padlocks and Other Locking Mechanisms"). Finding this piece of information tells you how one of the puzzles "resolves"—in other words, how it will end when it is solved. That can help you figure out which of the pieces it's connected to.

In the room, you'll look for something that can be unlocked, or maybe a place to enter a password. It might be a lock that's missing a key, a padlock with five digits, a number pad, a spinning dial, a computer screen.

The second part of this step is to ask, *What can I solve right now? And what should I come back to?*

Are there any areas where you have to insert or place an object, such as a shelf with markings, or a slot that a cartridge might fit into? These might be triggered by technology hidden inside the objects (see chapter 30 for notes on technology and electronics). Matching your collected items to these end points also helps you see how they might be solved.

For example, if you have two statues, but you find a shelf with three statue-shaped holes, you know that you'll probably have to place them on the shelves, in a certain order—but you can only do so once you find the third statue.

Many puzzles will be "gated" in this way.

A gate is a part of a puzzle design that restricts your access to further information or to an item that will advance you in a game. This stops you from picking up the final puzzle first, solving it immediately, and getting out of the room in under ten minutes.

If you can't find one piece of a puzzle, it's always a good idea to check over the room once more, just in case you overlooked something. Be sure to check high and low, and look inside every drawer, pocket, and potential hidey-hole.

And that reminds me: Pay attention to what reacts. Don't be afraid to push every button, flip every switch, and look in every drawer. (You'd be surprised by how many people don't look inside drawers!)

If you're pushing buttons, keep an eye—and an ear—on the rest of the room. Does anything react when you push it? That could be a light coming on (or turning off), a musical note playing . . .

If nothing reacts, remember to return to it later. It might not have been "on" at the time, but solving one puzzle might have activated it, allowing it to be solved. This is another form of gating, using electronics instead of a physical lock.

Again, remember: Communicate! If you find something, call it out. If you check a drawer and there's something inside, pull it out. If you think you might have overlooked something, call a person over to double-check your work.

And if you discover something inside one of those drawers, be sure you *remove it and place it in your collective items area.*

I have watched people open up a box, pick up and examine a key item—often what the entire group is searching for, although they don't know it yet—and place it back into the box, closing the lid after it.

Everyone saw that the one team member was looking in the box, so nobody thinks to look in it again. And they spend a great deal of time continuing to search, when in fact they had already found what they needed.

Teamwork makes the dream work.

Let's look at an example of solving using these principles:

Picture a briefcase. On the side of the briefcase is a logo, SUPER-HEROES INC.

In the room, someone has also found a drawer locked with a padlock.

Nearby, there's a folder with the same SUPERHEROES INC. logo. Inside the folder are two files with colored tabs. The tabs have numbers on them.

What do we know at this stage?

First, let's look more closely at the briefcase. It's locked with a three-digit lock. So we know our "solve" for that part of the puzzle is going to have three numbers.

On the outside of the briefcase, we see the SUPERHEROES INC. logo. The same logo that is on the folder.

That might mean they're connected, but it could also just be set decoration, especially if the logo appears in other places. It's important to not make assumptions that lead us down unproductive paths.

But for the sake of this example, let's say that the logo doesn't appear anywhere else in the room; it's only on these two items. So we can more or less assume that they're related.

Inside the folder are two files, one with a red tab, one with a yellow tab. On the red tab is a number 3, on the yellow tab is a number 2.

So now we know two important things:

First, these numbers are probably part of the three-digit solve to open the briefcase.

And second, we only have two of the three numbers that we need for that solve.

So now we can ask ourselves a couple of questions:

Do we have enough information to try to solve the puzzle? That depends.

Let's say that the tabs on the files are in different locations: the red one is near the top, and the yellow one near the bottom.

We can assume, then, that the third tab will be in the middle. This type of placement is not an accident, but a deliberate choice by the designers.

The briefcase lock is vertical:

0

0

0

So the numbers on the file tabs are probably telling us the order of the numbers, as they will be entered into the vertical briefcase lock.

That gives us the following:

3

?

2

We know that the answer to the missing number is on a third file, which is probably hidden in that locked drawer. But there's an opportunity to skip over that completely.

See that middle wheel? The numbers on it go from 0 to 9. Because we know the numbers on either side, a puzzle solver could spin the wheel to 0, try the lock, spin the wheel to 1, try the lock, and so on, until it unlocks, without getting that third piece of info.

This is called "brute-forcing" a puzzle. It can be very satisfying to figure out a puzzle this way, because in a way, you've beaten it. It can also be frustrating and confusing, depending on the rest of the group.

It's frustrating because it skips over a step—finding the key, unlocking the drawer, getting the number that way.

And it can be confusing to your teammates, because that drawer is still locked even though the solving has moved on, and they may have missed that step unfolding.

Talk about this with your group beforehand to see what people are comfortable with!

Okay, back to the folders. As a designer, you don't really want people to be able to brute-force a puzzle. So, let's take a step back and make the folders different. If we put the tabs at the same level on each folder, there's no immediately obvious indication of the order. Much better.

So, what is our next step in solving this puzzle?

We've assessed everything that's available to us currently, and tested what we were able to test. There's one piece of information that's unused so far: the locked drawer. So it's back to examine and gather.

We look around the room again and find a hidden key! Marvelous.

We open up the drawer and find the third file, with the third colored tab. This one is blue, and it has a number, 1.

So now we have three colors (red, yellow, blue), and three numbers (3, 2, 1). But we don't have an order to input them into the briefcase. Examine and gather again.

We look around the room, and someone notices that there are three light bulbs on the wall. They're turned off.

Earlier, someone noticed a light switch on the wall. They flipped it, but the overhead lights didn't turn on or off, so they ignored it at the time. But now, they remember it exists!

They flip it, and the light bulbs turn on, revealing that they are colored: left to right, the bulbs are red, yellow, and blue.

Aha! That's the missing piece. Now we know the order for the numbers: red file, yellow file, and blue file.

We spin the wheels on the briefcase lock, entering 3-2-1. The briefcase pops open, revealing . . . the next puzzle!

By examining, gathering, assessing, and testing, we're able to fill in the blank spots and move through the game. It's a great example of teamwork, ingenuity, and puzzle-solving. Feels good, doesn't it?

CHAPTER 21

Strategies for Communication and the Importance of Teamwork

One of the most fun things about escape rooms isn't the game itself but playing it with your friends.

That said, the environment can be tense! It's easy to get stressed out by the timer ticking down, or snap at someone because you're frustrated about a puzzle you're struggling to solve.

That's no fun. (And your friend might not like it much, either!) Luckily, with a bit of mindfulness, you can make sure you're still friends when you come out of the room.

Communication is the number one most important thing in group gaming, and it must be learned and practiced. Once you master it, you will be a cog in a well-oiled machine.

1. Be nice. This is a stressful environment for everyone. Don't snap, and if someone snaps at you, don't take it personally. Keeping the team energetic and happy is just as important as playing the game itself.
2. Check in, but don't hover. If you find yourself missing a piece, or without something to do, it's a good idea to walk around and see if anyone needs help. If you've been working

on something for a while without making progress, see if someone else wants to try their hand at solving it.

3. Call out when you find something, or when it opens. Are people in another room? Stick your head in and tell them what's just happened.

4. Assess. Constantly assess. What has been used? What's remaining? What needs to be solved? In an escape room, people split up and work on different things. The clue you need for the puzzle might be across the room, or you might be holding something that unlocks a box someone else is working on. Make it a habit to check in with your teammates regularly to keep the game flowing.

5. Double-check. It's always a good idea to have a second or third pair of eyes on something. It's easy to overlook something, so if you find that you're not making progress, don't be too quick to dismiss an area of the room or an item that might have been used already.

6. Hand it off. Have a piece of information that hasn't been used yet? See who else might need it, then hand it over and let it go. Trying to enter a code that just won't work? Ask someone to double-check your work, or to try putting the code in.

PRO TIPS FROM AN ESCAPE ROOM ENTHUSIAST

Errol Elumir is an escape room enthusiast who's played more than two hundred rooms and runs a podcast for enthusiasts called *Room Escape Divas*, with Mike Yuan, Ruby Yuan, and Manda Whitney. I asked him his top tips for new players, from the point of view of an escape room enthusiast.

His recommendations:

Never feel too proud to ask for a hint

"Enthusiasts have an internal clock to help us gauge how far we are in a room, and a newcomer probably wouldn't. I think a lot of enthusiasts will say, 'Okay, let's just ask for a hint.'

"If you spend more than five minutes on one puzzle and you can't get it at all, just ask for a helping hand. Sometimes something is broken, and it's not even your fault! Hints are there for a reason, so you shouldn't be dogged about not asking."

Practice swimming before you dive into the deep end of the pool

"Don't try and do all of the biggest escape rooms in your area first—wait until you get a few under your belt. You have to spend the time learning how escape rooms work, and you can focus on learning to work with your people.

"Get that out of the way, and then you can focus on the room. That's really the biggest advantage enthusiasts have over newcomers: we know how to work with each other, and we know what to expect in the room."

Get a regular team together

"Escape rooms can be expensive, and visiting hundreds of rooms requires a higher income bracket than normal. I have a nine-to-five job and I'm older, so that's advantageous. I'm also quite extroverted, so I'll just go in and introduce myself to a lot of people. I also talk about escape rooms a lot and find people that are interested.

"I think a lot of people start their own meetup group to find people to play with. Just find other people that are willing to talk to new people."

Communicate with your team

"If you find something, say something. When we play, we designate a table as the 'thing' table.

"Also, it's okay to be wrong in an escape room.

"I remember the first time we did an escape room, and one person in our group was a very good searcher. She was trying to put a code in, and she failed twice, and she thought, *You know what, I'm horrible at these, somebody else put the code in.*

"That was great, because she acknowledged the fact that she couldn't put it in, and she let somebody else do it instead of saying, *No, no, I'm going to put it in no matter how long it takes me.*

"Being able to give yourself that lenience that it's okay to not do something right away, and [knowing your strengths] to be able to give tasks to teammates who are good at them if you're not."

CHAPTER 22

How Hints Work

Hints are a big part of escape rooms, and it's important to know how they work and why you might want to use them while you're playing.

Different rooms have different methods of giving hints—it could be a person in the room, a wall-mounted screen that you can read, a conversation via walkie-talkie, passing notes through a door, or some other method.

WHAT IS A HINT?

Hints are small pieces of information provided to the players during gameplay.

Sometimes, the path to a puzzle's solution isn't going to be easy or clear. (After all, these are puzzles made by people, and no design is perfect.)

Hints exist to bridge the gap between the puzzle's design and the player's ability to interpret it.

TO HINT, OR NOT TO HINT?

Something I see all the time is people feeling that if they're asking for a hint, they're somehow failing themselves. So I want to emphasize: *Taking hints is a good thing.*

At the end of the day, you're playing these games to have fun. Frustration isn't fun! A good hint won't tell you the answer—after all, the game makers want you to solve everything yourself—but it will nudge you in the right direction, or tell you if you're totally off track so that you can course-correct.

That lets you get back to having as much fun as possible.

WHEN TO ASK FOR A HINT

I have a strategy for when to ask for a hint, and it's something that I discuss with my team beforehand, and that we all agree to in advance.

When I play games, if we've been working on a clue for five minutes with no progress, I ask for a hint. Sometimes I get stubborn and will wait seven minutes, even though I know that if it's been that long and I still haven't gotten it, it's very unlikely that I will be able to suddenly pull the solving method out of thin air.

Plus, it's important to keep the game flowing, and if a tiny nudge or redirection of attention is going to make that happen, I'm happy.

LISTEN TO YOUR BODY

Also, it's important to listen to your body while you're playing.

Are you feeling angry or frustrated? Do you want to get out—and not in the good way that brought you to an escape room in the first place?

Take a breather, walk around, stretch your arms.

And then ask for help. It's the game monitor's job to help you have as much fun as possible.

ASKING FOR HINTS WITHOUT SPOILERS

A hint isn't just revealing the answer. More often than not, it's just redirecting your attention to something you've overlooked.

There are ways to clarify what kind of hint you want. I've included some examples below:

"Help, we need a hint!"
It's fine to just ask for help. That's what the game monitor is for!

"Can you confirm that this information is correct?"
This is especially helpful if you have a code that you feel is right but doesn't seem to be working.

Knowing if the code is correct doesn't give you the answer to the puzzle, but it gives you a new set of information to work with: you may be entering the code incorrectly, or into the wrong place. The lock itself might be broken.

And if you find out that it's incorrect, you know to go back and work on the previous part of the puzzle again.

Either way, more information is what you need, and a hint will give it to you.

"Can you give us a nudge in the right direction?"

Sometimes, you'll be very close to an answer but unable to see how to get to it. A gentle redirection can make all the difference in the world. Plus you still get the satisfaction of solving it yourself.

"Have we missed something important?"

This one seems obvious, but it's very easy to get tunnel vision while playing a game. If you're feeling stuck and there's no clear way to move forward, asking to be pointed at the next thing can be enough to get you moving.

"Can we please have the answer?"

If you're at your wit's end, sometimes it's better to just move on. The key question to answer is, are you having fun? If not, there's no shame in asking to be moved on to the next part.

HINTS IN NON-LIVE GAMES

Because escape rooms come in many forms, you may have to look up hints for a board game or digital game. The hint system for different types of games will vary, so check beforehand, and be sure to agree with your team on a strategy for when you'll take hints.

Remember, you're there to have as much fun as possible, and hints are designed to help you do that.

CHAPTER 23

How to Solve
Any Escape Room Puzzle

So, puzzles. They're a big part of escape rooms (obviously!) but they can seem very intimidating if you've never solved one before.

Don't worry, though. Remember, every puzzle is designed to have a solution.

With a bit of practice, you'll be able to solve with the best of them.

HOW TO ATTACK ANY PUZZLE

You enter an escape room for the first time, or open a folder and see a huge group of image files. There are no instructions, so your job is to try to figure out how things are connected. Where do you even begin?

Look for patterns, and group things together. Are there any items that belong in a set together? Are there patterns that repeat over multiple items? Is there a set of images that looks like it might form a bigger picture?

Your goal is to sort out which things belong together so you can figure out what that means for the next step of solving.

For example, you might have a huge stack of playing cards. At first, they might seem random. But when you look closer, the backs of the cards have different colors: red, black, and blue.

So that's one way to begin dividing them into groups.

Let's say that you do that and realize that there are five cards in each set.

They look like this:

Red: 2, 4, 6, 8, 9

Black: 2, 4, 5, 6, 8

Blue: 2, 4, 5, 6, 7

There's obviously some kind of pattern . . . but what does it mean?

The next step is to assess what type of code you're dealing with.

RECOGNIZING CODES

If you're just starting out with puzzles, you might not recognize many codes at first. This is why practice is so important—after a while, you will be able to spot patterns, or the most common ways that puzzle designers try to hide things.

For example, a series of six shapes or dots in a two-by-three grid might mean it's a braille puzzle. Or a group of clocks could mean that the puzzle uses semaphore code. Check out chapter 25 about codes and ciphers to get a sense for how many different ways something might be encoded.

The code may not be immediately clear, so try and assess the puzzle with the other techniques, keeping in mind that you'll have to come back to this step.

SOLVING

With the card sets, you can see that the numbers are even or odd. You've used the numbers to place the cards into the correct order. So the next step is to abstract the information:

Red: even, even, even, even, odd

Black: even, even, odd, even, even

Blue: even, even, odd, even, odd

There are two "states" here (odd or even), so the code is likely to be one of two things that use two symbols: Morse code or binary code.

Each of these sets has five numbers in it, so it's unlikely to be Morse code, as those letters contain fewer parts. But each letter in binary code is made up of five digits.

So let's abstract the card information once more, looking at just the red card. It could be read in two ways: 11110 or 00001.

11110 isn't a letter in binary, but 00001 is! It translates to "A."

From this, we can assume that an even number is equal to a 0 and an odd number is equal to a 1.

That looks like:

Red: 00001 = A

Black: 00100 = C

Blue: 00101 = E

This spells out "ACE."

(By the way, no game is going to expect you to remember binary off the top of your head. If it wants you to use binary as a code, you should be able to find it on a code sheet or a chart somewhere in the game.)

ASSESSING YOUR INFORMATION

In this case, a natural next step would be to examine an ace card from the big, random pile and see what it might reveal, or to enter "ACE" as a password somewhere in the game.

Which brings me to the next step: think about the structure of the puzzle itself. What is the end goal of the puzzle?

Sometimes this will be obvious. You may have a padlock that has three letters, so you know you're going to be trying to come up with a three-letter word.

Sometimes, though, it will be less obvious. You may end up getting a number out of the puzzle, but until you write it down, you might not realize it has the same number of digits as a phone number.

This is why it's important to keep tabs on what has been used in a room so far, and what hasn't. If you know that there's a telephone in the room, but you haven't used it yet, it makes it much easier to connect the puzzle solution with the next step of dialing a number.

ORDERING

There are two other common techniques for solving that will help you untangle many puzzles. These are ordering and indexing.

In puzzle-solving, ordering is using any information that tells you what order to place individual puzzle components in so you can read them correctly as or after you solve them.

In the cards puzzle I've described, I gave the order as red, black, and blue, which is correct. But in an actual game, this may not be laid out as clearly.

But there's likely a clue about the order somewhere.

Let's look at different ways that ordering can be presented in a game, using the cards as the example.

There might be a visual that indicates the correct order. For example, three posters mounted to the wall, arranged in red-black-blue order, match the color of the cards. So you'll have to pay attention to these types of details so you can make that connection yourself.

Or you might have to guess it by unscrambling the letters.

This works in the cards puzzle, because there aren't many ways to combine the letters. The only options are CEA, CAE, EAC, ECA, AEC, and ACE.

The first five options are obviously not words, but "ACE" is. Hence, that is likely to be your answer.

In some games, you'll have much longer words, which are nearly impossible to unscramble yourself, at least not quickly, so again, the game should give you some sort of guidance in how to tackle the problem.

(Also, if you know the correct order, sometimes you can guess the end of a word without needing to solve the entire puzzle, saving you time. But that will only work if the letters aren't scrambled.)

INDEXING

Indexing is another way of getting letters out of a set of words.

For an indexing puzzle, you will usually find a list of numbers and words. To index the puzzle is to count the indicated number of letters into a word and select the letter you land on.

By doing this, you will get a set of letters that spell out a new word.

Let's set the cards to one side and use a different example.

Imagine that you're playing a virtual game. The avatar sends you a link to a recipe site, saying that they're looking for a good recipe for pumpkin pie.

You scroll down the site, finding the pumpkin pie recipe. There's only one, so this must be it . . . but the ingredients look very wrong.

This is the recipe on the site:

Ingredients

COOKIES (7)

PEANUTS (1)

PUMPKINS (6)

CREAM (1)

RICE (4)

Six pumpkins, one peanut? That can't be right . . . and it's not! This is an example of indexing.

Count the letters, and circle the letter indicated by the number at the end.

So the seventh letter of "COOKIES" is "S." The first letter of "PEA-NUTS" is "P." And so on, down the line, until you spell out "SPICE."

This is a very common puzzle mechanic, and one that you are likely to see frequently, so remember to look out for it.

Other types of indexing might send you to a certain word (the first word of every sentence in a long paragraph, for example), or might even be a book cipher that directs you to look at a certain page, paragraph, and word within that paragraph.

And here's another tip: if you think you might know the answer, go ahead and enter it. There's no penalty for trying a number on a padlock, for example. (A game should warn you if there is some sort of penalty attached.)

A lot of people are hesitant to enter something until they feel 100 percent convinced that it is correct. But in puzzle-solving, your goal is always to get more information. Trying a guess in the lock gives you information, even if it isn't the right answer.

CHAPTER 24

Padlocks and Other Locking Mechanisms

One thing I like to tell people is, "There are only so many ways to lock a box."

In a real-world space, when you really don't want someone to get into a drawer, there are only a few ways to keep them out. (The same applies to ways of hiding information, but we'll discuss that in the chapters on common codes and types of puzzles.)

And in a digital space, there are similar limitations.

Once you learn to recognize the way things are locked, you'll be able to identify your goal and work backward from there.

These are the most common types of locks you'll encounter in an escape room, whether it's in-person or virtual.

LOCK AND KEY

Keys are items that can be inserted into a lock to release it. Most commonly, these are keys and locks just like the ones you'd see on the door to a house.

In these, the lock has a series of pins and springs. The pins are suspended at different heights. When the correct key is inserted, the lock's pins are raised to the same height, which allows the cylinder inside to turn.

In an escape room, there are many clever ways to use the same principle—an object with incisions that raise up corresponding pieces—to unlock a puzzle. Keep an eye out for objects made of wood or plastic that look like they could be inserted into other objects.

PADLOCKS

Padlocks are another common feature of many escape rooms. They are locks with a latch and a bolt that is released when the correct password is input.

There are many different types, including:

CIRCULAR DIAL

The classic padlock—one you've likely used to secure your bike, locker, or storage space over the years.

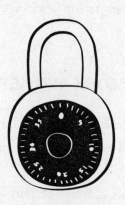

NUMBERS

These padlocks use spinning wheels to input numbers. Be aware that on many locks of this type, you read the numbers along the thin side of the lock.

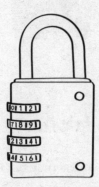

To check to make sure you're looking at the right section, see if the numbers on the padlock have been set to zeroes by the game attendant during the game reset.

Sometimes the lock will have a mark on it, like an arrow or colored stripe, that tells you where to enter the number. If you're entering it into one set of "windows" but it isn't working, try the next one, just to be sure. And as always, if you're stuck, ask your game monitor for confirmation.

LETTERS

Letter locks are a lot of fun because they mean puzzles can resolve to a word. These usually work with vertically spinning wheels. Again, be sure to check that the letters are aligned correctly, and give the lock a firm tug to open it.

DIRECTIONAL

Directional locks seem really cool at first, but in reality they're a tough nut to crack. First, they can get pretty sticky and stop working in the room, which obviously ruins the fun! Second, once you've tried a combination, if it's not correct, the lock has to be reset before you can enter a new one.

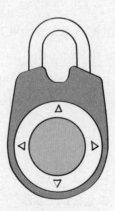

How directional locks are reset:

Enter the wrong combo? The reset for the most common version of these locks is easy. Hold the lock in your hand and press down on the latch twice. *Click-click.* Voilà! Totally reset.

Some in-person escape rooms will have a set of padlocks in the lobby for you to play with before you go into your game room. It's a good idea to try things like these resets when they're offered, so it doesn't slow you down when you're in the room with the timer running.

PUSH-BUTTON

Push-button locks are exactly what they sound like. You enter the combination by pushing numbered buttons in the right order.

As always, if it's feeling sticky, or if you're convinced that you have the right answer but it just won't open, ask your game monitor to confirm the solve, or to enter it into the padlock for you if you can't seem to make it work.

DEAD BOLT

A dead bolt is a locking mechanism used on many residential doors. It works by inserting a solid piece of metal into a receiving end, when a key is turned.

ELECTROMAGNETIC LOCK

As escape rooms evolved, designers took a look around and started asking themselves, *How can we use fewer padlocks but still keep stuff locked away?* Enter electromagnets.

Electromagnets are two-part magnets that turn "on" or "off" when an electric current is run through them (or removed from them).

Because electromagnets are found on the insides of containers, instead of the outside where players can see them, it's a great way to hide a panel in a wall, or keep a door closed without revealing that it's locked.

As you get more experience with escape rooms, you'll be able to spot places in a room that are likely to contain electromagnets, such as a door or cabinet with no obvious external latch.

Pro tip: if you happen to see one, remember where it is, but consider whether you want to tell other team members. (This is something that you can discuss as you figure out your team strategy, as described in chapter 14, "What to Know Before You Go.")

If you choose to not tell them, remember that it's not to keep a secret from your teammates but to avoid spoilers and preserve the element of surprise. Keep the location of the hidden lock in mind, and if someone solves a puzzle later but can't figure out if something opened, you'll know at least one more place to check.

LOCKBOX

A lockbox is a small container that is opened with a code, sometimes using a number pad or a small spinning lock.

CRYPTEX

A cryptex is a type of lockbox. It has a cylinder surrounded by spinning wheels, and when the wheels are aligned, one end of the cylinder can be removed, revealing a hollow interior.

The word "cryptex" was created for the 2003 book *The Da Vinci Code* by Dan Brown. It is a combination of the Greek κρυπτός, *kryptós*, meaning "hidden" or "secret," and the Latin *caudex*, meaning "trunk of a tree" or "block of wood."[1]

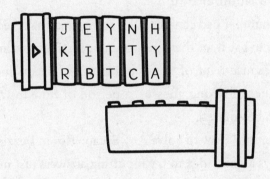

SAFE

Who doesn't want to feel like a safecracking hero in a spy movie? Safes are a fun addition to any escape room, but there are some special conditions that players should be aware of.

Safes with a Spinning Dial

Most of the time, safes with a spinning dial are going to follow similar rules to the dial padlock, so as long as you're familiar with that, you're good to go.

In other cases, the safes or locks might be old. In that situation, the game monitor might have briefed you about how the lock works, or you might find instructions in the room.

Even with clear instructions, old locks can be very fiddly, so if you think you know the right combination but it's just not going in right, or the safe won't open, be sure to 1) ask the game monitor to confirm that the answer is correct, and if it is, 2) ask them for help entering it in.

Safes with a Number Pad

Safes with a number pad can be tricky, so you may have received instructions on how to use it, or there may even be instructions in the room.

That's because a lot of these digital safes have a "lockout" after a certain number of wrong guesses, a period of time in which no more numbers can be entered.

In chapter 23, "How to Solve Any Escape Room Puzzle," you learned that it's always a good idea to try inputting answers just in case, because there's no penalty for trying and getting it wrong. Digital safes are the exception to this rule, which is all the more reason to use the guidance at your disposal.

NUMBER PAD

Number pads are a way of entering a numerical code into a lockbox, digital device, or other mechanism. They are usually rectangular grids of numbers, like a touch pad you would use to enter a restricted building.

Number pads are also commonly used in puzzles, so keep this in mind if you encounter them. (See also chapter 26: "Types of Puzzles").

OTHER LOCKING MECHANISMS

Hidden Doors

Hidden doors are a fun feature of escape rooms. Just think how exciting it is to push a button and suddenly a hole in the wall opens up, with more puzzles beckoning beyond!

If you look carefully, you'll be able to spot some of these hidden doors. In some cases, you might guess that something's hidden but realize later it was just your imagination. And in others, you'll never see them coming.

As always, think about whether you want to spoil the "reveal" for the rest of your group, should you discover one before it opens. But since the goal is to sketch a thorough map of the game and the space it occupies, looking for potential places that the space might expand is part of play.

So, how do you recognize these portals?

One, look for irregular architecture. Are you starting out in a tiny space that seems like it couldn't possibly hold an hour's worth of a game? Are there suspiciously shaped pieces of furniture? There's no guarantee that these are hidden doors, but there's a good chance.

Two, look for things that are, well, door-size. Doors aren't all the exact same size, but generally the standard is thirty-six inches (three feet) wide by eighty inches (six feet eight inches) tall. Bookcases, cabinets, seven-foot-tall framed posters . . . all these may be hiding a door behind them.

Some escape rooms include crawl spaces, too. I've scooted through more fireplaces with false backs than I can count. (Okay, that's not exactly true—it's four.)

Again, the presence of a tall poster or a fireplace isn't a guarantee that there's a space behind it. But there's a good chance, so definitely keep it in mind when you're sketching your mental map.

Unusual and Custom Locks

Sometimes escape rooms get very creative with how they lock things away! You might encounter something like a lock hidden behind a piece of wood, which is opened by sliding a magnet along the surface, catching and pulling the invisible latch.

Or you might be asked to pull a rope that tugs on a latch out of sight, or overhead.

Whatever the case, it's sure to be interesting. And if you can't figure it out, ask your game monitor for an assist.

Computer Passwords

You might encounter a computer, email system, or password-protected telephone voice mail in an escape room or virtual game.

There are a lot of ways to conceal a password like this, but it doesn't hurt to start by entering words that are close by—you never know, the fictional character might just keep their password written on a sticky note by their desk!

However, these systems might also have a time-out or other penalty for entering a wrong answer, so don't mash the keyboard, either.

Locks in Virtual Games

If you're playing a virtual game, you'll use padlocks and other mechanisms the same way you would if you were physically in the room yourself, but without the hassle of sticky locks or keys that don't quite fit right.

In a virtual game that uses websites, images, and other files, you're likely to encounter clear "gates" that serve to lock away information. These might be things like password-protected files or log-in forms.

You might also encounter things that transcend the computer, like having to call a number and enter a password that way.

And finally, you may need to give a verbal instruction or password to move the game along.

When in doubt, ask the attendant watching your game for guidance.

———————

Padlocks and hidden doors are just a few of the clever ways people conceal things in escape rooms. The world of codes and puzzle design is a vast and intriguing one.

CHAPTER 25

Common Codes and Ciphers

As I said in the previous chapter, "There are only so many ways to lock a box."

That's true for physical locks, but it's also true for ways of concealing information. When it's done by translating the information into another *thing*, it's called "encoding" or "encipherment."

The following are the most common types of codes that you might encounter in an escape room or puzzle game. There are of course more codes out there, but an understanding of these will get you pretty far.

You'll notice that many of these can hide information through the use of symbols or other images. You will find it very helpful to become familiar with the patterns that these codes make, so that when you come upon their "encoded" form, you'll recognize what you're dealing with.

LETTER-FINDING

Sometimes letters might be concealed in a note, mural, or artwork.

Look at the text (or other characters) closely. Are any letters bold, capitalized, underlined, or otherwise marked to stand out? Try writing them out in order to see if they spell anything. Remember, it could be top to bottom, or left to right!

There's a message hidden in this note. Can you read it?

PLEASE REMEMBER TO PICK THIS FLOWER

SUBSTITUTION CIPHERS

Alphanumeric

You're probably already familiar with the concept of an alphanumeric encoding, which assigns a number to a letter of the alphabet.

If you assign a number to every letter in the alphabet, in order, you get A = 1, B = 2, C = 3, and so on, until Z = 26.

Let's translate the word "AYE" into numbers.

Here's a handy list.

A = 1	J = 10
B = 2	K = 11
C = 3	L = 12
D = 4	M = 13
E = 5	N = 14
F = 6	O = 15
G = 7	P = 16
H = 8	Q = 17
I = 9	R = 18

S = 19	W = 23
T = 20	X = 24
U = 21	Y = 25
V = 22	Z = 26

Using this table, we can write AYE as 1-25-5.

By the way, it's important to note the separation of numbers there. If I wrote 1255, I could mean 1-2-5-5 (ABEE), or 12-5-5 (LEE). Without the separation, there's no way to know for sure. If you find yourself in this situation, you can at least eliminate 55 as an option, since there's no fifty-fifth letter. That gives you three options to try (AYE, ABEE, LEE), although of course the one that forms an actual word should be the first on your list.

What do these numbers spell? 13-1-18-2-12-5

Caesar and Shift Ciphers

If you want to make the alphanumeric cipher harder, you still assign numbers to letters, in order, but this time you shift them.

In a regular alphanumeric cipher, A = 1, B = 2, and so on.

But if you shift the numbers by one, the assignment changes. So A = 2, B = 3, C = 4, et cetera.

You're less likely to find this in an escape room, but it does show up in many puzzle games, so it's useful to learn. This is called a shift cipher.

You can also assign letters to other letters. This type of encoding is known as a Caesar cipher. It might be written as "ROT-13," for "rotate by 13 places." (The 13 can be replaced by any number, but 13 is the most commonly used one by default.)

"ROT-13" means you would shift the alphabet thirteen spaces, and use that as your reference for decoding.

For example:

A = N	N = A
B = O	O = B
C = P	P = C
D = Q	Q = D
E = R	R = E
F = S	S = F
G = T	T = G
H = U	U = H
I = V	V = I
J = W	W = J
K = X	X = K
L = Y	Y = L
M = Z	Z = M

Here, using ROT-13 on the word "SHIFT" would encode it into the word "FUVSG."

MORSE CODE

Morse code was invented by Samuel Morse in the 1840s. Morse created the telegraph as a way to send messages between two points. A telegraph machine sends an electrical pulse along a wire, which is received by a machine on the other end. These pulses can be short or long. This is drawn out as dots (short) or dashes (long). Each corresponds to a letter of the alphabet or a number.

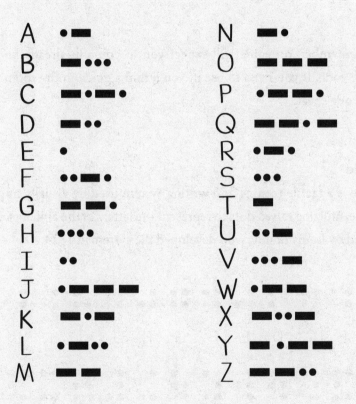

In a puzzle, Morse code can be concealed in many ways. It could be a pattern of flashing lights or a series of vibrating pulses. Here's another example:

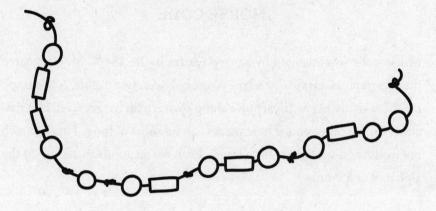

Remember, no game will expect you to come in already knowing Morse code. If you need to use it, you'll find a guide in the room or on your code sheet.

Braille

Braille is a tactile reading and writing system used by visually impaired people, utilizing raised dots to represent the letters of the alphabet. It was created by Louis Braille, who developed the system in 1824.

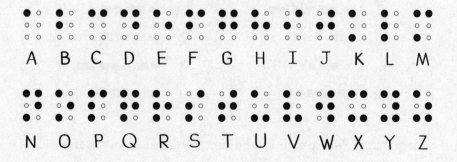

BINARY

Binary code is a two-symbol system used by computers in which numbers can be converted to letters, using combinations of 1s and 0s.[*] (Computer wires can be powered either "on" or "off.") When the numbers are strung together, they're read as letters or numbers. For example, 00010 (off-off-off-on-off) is "B"

A = 00001	N = 01110
B = 00010	O = 01111
C = 00011	P = 10000
D = 00100	Q = 10001
E = 00101	R = 10010
F = 00110	S = 10011
G = 00111	T = 10100
H = 01000	U = 10101
I = 01001	V = 10110
J = 01010	W = 10111
K = 01011	X = 11000
L = 01100	Y = 11001
M = 01101	Z = 11010

---

[*]This is called a "base 2" system because it uses two numbers. Decimal, which we use every day, is "base 10" because it uses ten numbers, the numbers 0 through 9. This is the stuff of way more complex puzzle-solving than your typical escape room, but it's an interesting fact all the same!

You can recognize a binary code by looking for a set of five symbols, composed of two different symbols.

For example:

ABBAA = 01100. That means ABBAA is "L."

Can you solve this puzzle?

INDEXING

"Indexing" is a term for extracting a letter from a word based on information given in the puzzle. Often the information is a number in parentheses after the word you must "index into."

For example, take a look at this set of words and numbers:

Apple (1)

Object (2)

Locked (3)

This is instructing you to count the letters in the words, according to the number. So:

Apple (1) means look at the first letter of the word "Apple." You get "A."

Object (2) means look at the second letter of the word "Object." You get "B."

See how it works?

If you see a set of words and a list of numbers, you might be looking at indexing.

Can you solve the indexing puzzle in this recipe?

Ingredients

13 drops of vanilla extract

4 tablespoons of sugar

3 teaspoons of baking powder

4 cups of water

What comes out of this recipe? (When you solve the puzzle, not when you actually try this concoction in real life, of course.)

Start by figuring out which section of the available text you're supposed to index into.

If the letters you're finding don't seem to be making a word, it's probable that you're off track, and need to try a different approach.

ACROSTIC

In an acrostic puzzle, the first letter of a set of words spells out the answer to the puzzle. That could be a sentence, paragraph, or any other grouping.

Here is a selection from a famous acrostic poem by the English poet John Keats. Can you read the name that it spells out?

Give me your patience, sister, while I frame
Exact in capitals your golden name;
Or sue the fair Apollo and he will
Rouse from his heavy slumber and instill
Great love in me for thee and Poesy.
Imagine not that greatest mastery
And kingdom over all the Realms of verse,
Nears more to heaven in aught, than when we nurse
And surety give to love and Brotherhood.

BOOK CIPHER

A book cipher is a fun way to make a code that's very personal to someone, since it relies on having a specific edition of a specific book.

This cipher is usually presented as a series of numbers, like 1-4-24-3. That means "chapter 1, paragraph 4, word 24, letter 3."

Because you're only getting one letter out of each set of numbers, it's easy to recognize this cipher in an escape room, because it will probably have a lot of numbers all together.

Here's a little cipher using the chapters of this book. Try and solve it!

1.6.11 / 7.2.39 / 1.1.11 / 1.1.12 / 15.26.4 / 15.26.5

ALBERTI DISK

The Alberti disk is a cipher wheel designed in 1467 by Leon Battista Alberti.

This cipher wheel has an outer ring and an inner ring, connected in the center. Along the outer ring is the alphabet, A through Z. The inner ring, which also has the alphabet, spins.

The wheel works by spinning the inner ring to align a letter with one on the outer ring.

These are fun to make at home; all you need are two pieces of paper, some scissors, and something to write with.

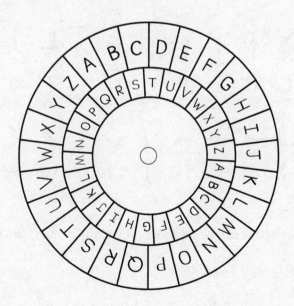

HIEROGLYPHICS

Hieroglyphics are symbol alphabets. You're probably familiar with Egyptian hieroglyphics, but in a creative fantasy world, these might also be runes or an alien script.

These will often make one symbol translate to one letter, when in real life they would translate to a more complex series of letters, but that's a bit too complicated for players in an hour-long experience, so we'll give them a bit of leeway.

SEMAPHORE

Semaphore is a naval flag communication system. A person stands holding two flags, and the position of their arms indicates a letter of the alphabet. It's a fantastic way to signal across a distance (like from one boat to another), but there are also plenty of ways it can be used for puzzles.

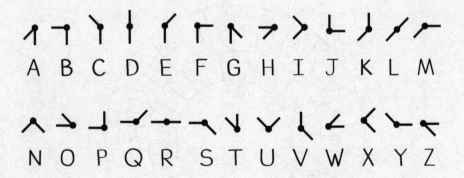

Semaphore code can be represented visually in many fun ways:

This spells "HELLO."

Fundamentally, the information you're seeking is the position of the lines. It may appear in many different forms, but now you'll be able to recognize the foundations of it and see through the picture.

Try it yourself here:

NAUTICAL FLAGS

At sea, ships use a system of flags and codes to communicate with each other at a distance.

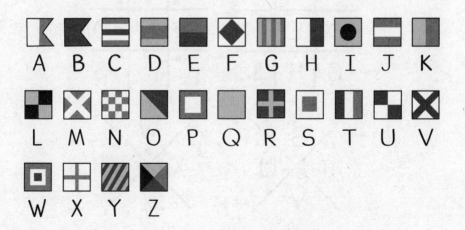

PIGPEN

Pigpen is a visual substitution code. Letters are represented by geometric shapes. The shapes are part of a larger grid.

If you see symbols that look like this, you're dealing with pigpen:

These symbols are based on the placement of letters into several diagrams, as seen here.

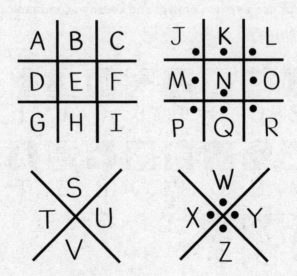

Try translating this message:

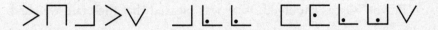

NATO ALPHABET

The NATO alphabet is a phonetic alphabet used in oral communication, such as over the radio. Each word stands for its initial letter.

A = Alfa	N = November
B = Bravo	O = Oscar
C = Charlie	P = Papa
D = Delta	Q = Quebec
E = Echo	R = Romeo
F = Foxtrot	S = Sierra
G = Golf	T = Tango
H = Hotel	U = Uniform
I = India	V = Victor
J = Juliett	W = Whiskey
K = Kilo	X = X-ray
L = Lima	Y = Yankee
M = Mike	Z = Zulu

Here's an example of how the NATO alphabet might be encoded into a sentence. Can you solve it, using the list provided?

"Bravo!" Oscar shouted. Oscar was pleased that the crate weighed under a kilo.

CHAPTER 26

Types of Puzzles

There are many different types of puzzles and ways of encoding information. Let's look at some you might encounter in an escape room, including examples of how they might be implemented.

This may seem like a long list, but once you get your puzzle glasses on, you'll start to recognize their essential elements no matter how they're dressed up, or how many types of codes are combined in them.

WORDPLAY

Wordplay puzzles can be a lot of fun. There are many varieties of how we can play with language, but here are a few common types you might come across.

Compound Word Chain

A compound word chain puzzle asks you to take compound words, or words with two parts, and combine them with other compound words, matching the end of one to the start of the next.

For example:

DAYLIGHT

LIGHTHOUSE

HOUSEWORK

WORKDAY

Drop-Down Letters

In these puzzles, you are usually given one word at the top of a grid and must transform it by moving it through a series of lines and spaces to reach a final answer. In some, like the example here, you may have to add or subtract a letter to get to the answer.

H A R D

_ _ _ _

C _ _ _

_ _ S _

_ _ _ _

E A S Y

FOLDING

In a folding puzzle, players fold or manipulate something, usually paper, in order to align marks or illustrations, or otherwise discover or reveal information.

This piece of paper must be folded in order.

When the folds are made according to instruction, marks on the paper align to reveal an answer.

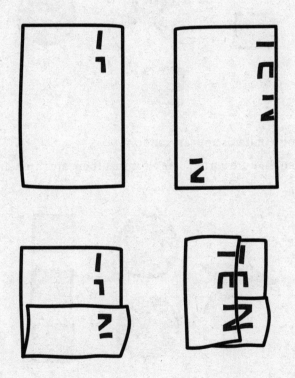

COUNTING

A counting puzzle requires the player to count the total number of items present.

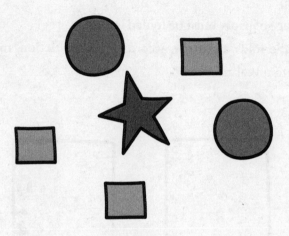

This group of items appears random.
But when they are sorted, it is clear that there are three shapes.

Counting the number of each shape gives a code: 1 = star, 2 = circle, 3 = square. This information may now be used elsewhere.

REFLECTION

A reflection puzzle utilizes mirrors or other reflective surfaces to manipulate or warp an image.

Taken alone, the markings on this page seem random. But when you mirror them, the message is revealed:

SCYTALE CIPHER

A scytale puzzle consists of a cylinder and a strip of material, often paper or cloth. The material is wrapped around the cylinder, and the result is readable.

There are two cylinders of different widths, and a ribbon with letters on it.

Wrapping the first cylinder reveals nothing legible. Wrapping the second cylinder reveals a word.

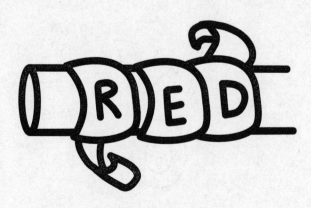

PAIRING/DRAWING LINES BETWEEN MATCHING THINGS TO OVERLAP A LETTER

For these puzzles, players make connections between pairs or sets of corresponding things. When they draw a line between the pairs, it intersects with a piece of information, such as a letter, number, or location on a map, giving the next part of the puzzle.

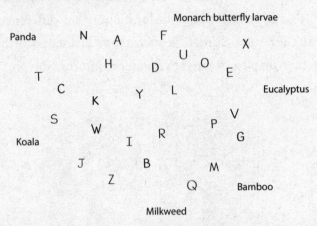

Here, people make the connection between animals and what they eat. When the lines are drawn between the pairs, each line intersects with only one letter.

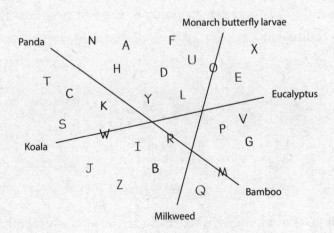

These letters spell out "W-O-R-M." Following the logic of the pairs (animals + what they eat), the answer is "BIRD."

SPOT-THE-DIFFERENCE

In a spot-the-difference puzzle, players compare two things, often versions of the same image, to note the locations of any differences between them. With these puzzles, there is often a third element, which the differences can then map to, in order to find more information or discover the next clue.

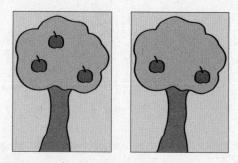

There is one difference between these two images.

We can take the location of the difference and map it to a third image. Note that the third image matches up to the first two, even though its content is different.

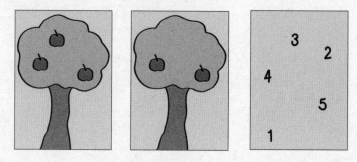

This gives us a number, which may then be used with another puzzle.

HOMOPHONE

A homophone is when the same pronunciation is used for two or more words. They may sound like something else when read or spoken aloud. In a puzzle it may be written in text form or represented visually (in which case it is also called a "Rebus").

Say this sentence out loud: *The bee can see the blue jay with its eye. Why are you watching?*

Several of the words can be written as single letters:

Bee = B	Why = Y
See = C	Are = R
Jay = J	You = U
Eye = I	

Some of these are more obvious than others. ("Why" equaling "Y" is a little tricky, in my opinion.)

PUT-TOGETHER

A put-together puzzle is any type of puzzle where the player is assembling something, whether it's flat like a jigsaw, or 3D like a Jenga tower.

A jigsaw puzzle is a familiar type of put-together puzzle. We know from the colors and images which pieces might fit together, even if we aren't given a guiding image to work from.

Tangram

Tangrams are a type of put-together puzzle. In a tangram, the player is given multiple pieces, all of which must fit together inside a frame or shape. The pieces may be flipped or rotated until they fit.

Players find a frame in a particular shape, as well as a set of pieces that seem to go together.

Assembling the pieces doesn't seem to make any sense.

But when the pieces are correctly inserted into the frame, the answer is revealed.

TAKE-APART

A take-apart puzzle is one that requires the player to disassemble something. These often use mechanical tricks or secret compartments.

Puzzle boxes appear to have no openings, handles, or latches.

But if the panels are slid in a specific order, the box opens to reveal an inner compartment.

INTERLOCKING

Interlocking puzzles, also known as Burr puzzles, consist of several pieces, often notched, which combine to form a 3D object.

CHESS

These puzzles are based on the board game chess. In a normal game of chess, players take turns moving the pieces according to a set of specific rules.

The most common element that can be taken from chess and repurposed for puzzles is the way each piece moves on the chessboard. Those moves are:

Pawn: moves one space at a time, vertically or horizontally.

Queen: moves any number of spaces, in any direction, vertically, horizontally, or diagonally.

King: moves one space at a time, vertically, horizontally, or di-agonally.

Bishop: Moves any number of spaces, diagonally.

Rook: moves any number of spaces, vertically or horizontally.

Knight: moves in an L-shaped pattern.

Another form these might take is the Tour puzzle.

Tour Puzzle

In a tour puzzle, players move around a grid, from one letter to the next, according to a given set of rules. These often utilize elements of chess.

For example, a player might need to use the knight's movement rule to go from letter to letter. This is called a "Knight's Tour" puzzle.

WORD SEARCH

You're probably familiar with word searches, but just in case, these are grids of letters consisting of hidden words. There can be additional layers of puzzle beyond the initial "find a word" task.

SUDOKU

Sudoku is a logic-based number-placement puzzle. Solvers must fill in a grid based on rules, such as each row, column, and square may have only one instance of each number 1 through 9.

5	3			7				
6			1	9	5			
	9	8					6	
8				6				3
4			8		3			1
7				2				6
	6					2	8	
			4	1	9			5
				8			7	9

DETANGLING

These puzzles require the player to connect or disconnect its parts from one another.

A familiar example is the bent-nail puzzle, which appears to be two nails, both folded, and apparently inseparable.

To solve the nail puzzle, the player must twist and turn the parts in a specific manner to separate the two entwined pieces.

DISSECTION OR CUTTING

A cutting puzzle requires the player to make a series of cuts or marks, usually on paper, which then reveals an answer.

This piece of paper may be folded along the dotted lines. When cuts are made to the indicated lines, pieces of the paper may be removed.

When the paper is unfolded, the holes now form the shapes of letters.

(Most escape rooms won't expect you to destroy items unless you are specifically instructed to do so.)

PLANK

Plank puzzles are logic games that ask the solver to use logs or planks of predetermined length to make their way across a grid, usually containing obstacles.

SEQUENTIAL MOVEMENT

To solve sequential movement puzzles, the player must physically move pieces around, either in a specific order or in strategic sequences until the puzzle is solved. This category includes multiple other types of puzzles, including pathfinding and labyrinths.

DEXTERITY

These puzzles require physical skills or manual dexterity to solve them. For example, a labyrinth puzzle might have raised ridges forming a series of channels.

To solve this type of puzzle, the player may hold the labyrinth in their hand and tilt it back and forth, carefully maneuvering a ball bearing toward the end goal.

PATH-FOLLOWING

To solve these puzzles, the player must follow a specific route.

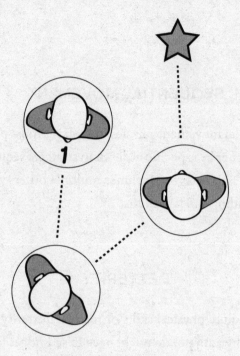

Here, the player examines the eyes of the statues, following the direction they're pointing until they reach a final location.

ANAGRAM

An anagram is a word scramble that creates a new word or phrase.

For example, the letters in "astronomer" may be rearranged to form the words "moon starer."

REBUS

A rebus is a puzzle that uses pictures, and the way the items in those pictures sound when spoken aloud, to form words.

Can you solve this one?

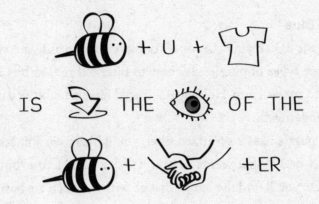

OPENING

These puzzles are defined by the need to open, close, or undo the object. Types include boxes and bags closed with padlocks that open with a key or code.

HIDDEN PICTURE (FILTER)

You might come across a hidden picture puzzle that uses a filter.

Have you ever seen those 3D cinema glasses, where one lens is blue and one is red? These work on the same principle.

An image is printed with many colors layered over one another. The image part of the puzzle will usually look like a mess of colors and textures.

But when it's viewed through the colored lens, the matching color in the print becomes invisible, revealing the image underneath.

Sometimes this effect is achieved with a polarized lens and a digital screen, or with colored lights rather than a physical lens.

Red and Blue

Those classic 3D cinema glasses, if you have a pair handy, are very helpful for these types of puzzles. It's easy to filter out red, so this is a common way to conceal info. Holding up the red filter reveals the darker blue printing underneath.

If the puzzle uses a polarized filter, you'll likely see a lit screen, like a computer or TV, that seems to have a flicker of a picture, but nothing obvious. Or, you'll find the lenses that go with it, which are basically just regular polarized sunglasses.

Remember that some puzzles will get clever and *combine* lens colors for additional filtering!

HOLDING UP TO THE LIGHT

Some puzzles may be printed in such a way that they are only visible when held up to the light, like a watermark on paper or a security measure in paper currency.

TEMPERATURE

Some papers and inks have special properties and are reactive to heat or cold.

For example, invisible inks such as lemon juice, which are invisible when they dry on paper, will turn brown when held up to a heat source like a light bulb.

BLACKLIGHT REVEAL

A favorite method for hiding info in escape rooms is the blacklight puzzle. These types of puzzles use UV (ultraviolet) light to reveal symbols or text written in transparent paint. When the light shines on it, it fluoresces, becoming visible.

OVERLAYS

In a game environment, pay attention to items that are the same size, especially pieces of paper and other flat surfaces. Some puzzles require you to layer parts, or to put a sheet of paper over something so that it can highlight information on the surface it covers.

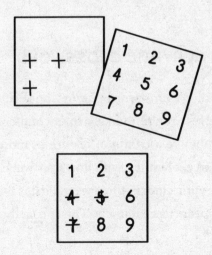

CAMERA-BASED

If you come upon a camera feed in a game, watch it for a while to see if it changes. You may need to pay attention to people or objects passing in and out of the field of view. If it's part of a closed-circuit TV system (CCTV), you may be able to switch between various camera views.

JIGSAW

A jigsaw is a type of put-together puzzle. Fun fact: the first jigsaw puzzles were created in the 1760s and have been popular ever since!

CROSSWORD

Crossword puzzles generally have lists of clues and a blank grid that must be filled in using the clues. Sometimes these puzzles are presented without the grid, significantly increasing the difficulty of solving the overall puzzle.

CRYPTIC CROSSWORD

A cryptic crossword is a crossword puzzle whose clues are also smaller puzzles in themselves. You're unlikely to encounter them in a regular escape room, but they're a common feature in more advanced puzzle hunts, so it's good to get familiar with how they work.

You can read cryptic clues in three ways. First is the "surface reading," which is what it appears to be initially. This is usually not relevant to the actual puzzle.

Next is the "definition," the clue that tells you something about the word you're looking for.

Finally, there's the "wordplay." This is a set of information that hints about how to solve the trick.

Just like in a regular crossword puzzle, there is a set of commonly used words that suggest a specific clue. One example is "flower." Initially, that looks like the word for a thing that grows in a garden and has petals.

But if you read it in a different way, it becomes "flow-er," or "a thing that flows," like a river.

Half the battle in solving cryptics is getting to know that list!

LOGIC-ORDERING

This type of puzzle asks the player to follow a set of logical rules to determine the order of something.

You can recognize these because there will be a list of some kind that suggests an order.

For example: "The fox was loaded onto the boat before the third animal."

In an escape room, these might be accompanied by a grid to help the player keep things straight as they solve. Alternately, you may have to create the grid yourself on paper or on a whiteboard.

SHADOW

Shadow puzzles are physical objects that, when correctly assembled or aligned, throw a shadow that reveals the answer.

ALIGNMENT

Alignment puzzles are visual challenges. Sometimes it means standing in the right place in the room to see the edge of a picture as it lines up with an image on the wall.

Here's a common visual puzzle you'll see printed in books. Can you figure out how to read it?

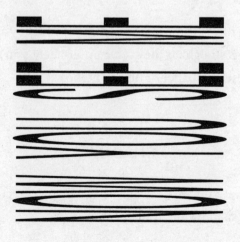

CYLINDER MIRROR

This is a type of alignment puzzle and is a reflective puzzle. But unlike mirror puzzles, which align the image using just one straight edge, these can be read using a cylinder to unwarp the image.

BOOK-EDGE

A book-edge puzzle is an image printed along the thin edge of the pieces of paper that make up a book. The image becomes visible when the pages are fanned. This is also known as a fore-edge painting and was originally popularized in the early 1700s.

NUMBER PADS

Number pads are a method of entering numbers into a mechanism. They may be part of a lock that you're supposed to solve, but they are also commonly featured in puzzles.

One common method for incorporating a number pad is to use the combination of digits and letters found on a telephone.

For example, if you found a phone and the numbers "2-1" were written next to it, it might be pointing at the letter "A," the first letter on the number 2 button. It follows that "B" would be 2-2, and "C" would be 2-3. Using this method, we can easily form words or sentences.

Can you solve the puzzle here, using a keypad from a telephone?

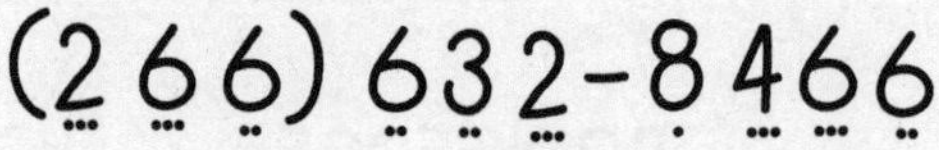

(2̤ 6̤ 6̤) 6̤3̤2̤-8̤ 4̤6̤6̤

NONOGRAMS

A nonogram (also known as a "picross") is a logic puzzle. Using numbers along the edges of the puzzle, spaces in a grid are colored in to form a picture.

The numbers on the edge of the puzzle indicate how many squares in that row or column are filled in or left blank.

Can you solve the nonogram puzzle here to discover a number?

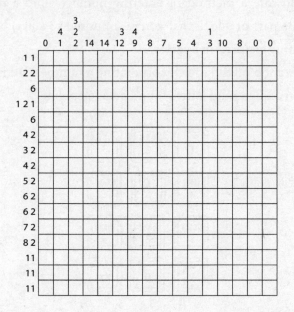

MAZE

Maze puzzles are considered "path puzzles," as the player traces a path among a set of lines, avoiding dead ends, to reach an end point.

MAGNET

A magnet puzzle is a puzzle where the player uses a magnet to move an object along a channel or pipe. You can recognize these types of puzzles in two ways. First, if there's a metallic object trapped inside something that is too deep to reach into, it's most likely a magnet puzzle. Sometimes these will have a transparent window so that you can see the object's location, even if you can't reach it.

Second, if you have a magnet, especially on a stick, but aren't sure what it's used for, an object may be concealed somewhere that requires you to use the magnet to retrieve it. Time to look for potential hiding places!

ELECTRIC-EDGE

Have you ever played the board game Operation? In that game, players use tweezers to very carefully lift small plastic pieces out of holes lined with metal. If the metal tweezers touch the metal edge of the hole, the game buzzes, and the player has to stop.

Electric-edge puzzles work in the same way. Often they take the form of a metal ring around a curved metal pole. The player has to manipulate the ring around the pole without them coming into contact, or else the puzzle will restart. I've seen these in many sizes: sometimes a picture on a wall, sometimes built to fill a whole room. You can check whether the puzzle is active by touching the metal parts together to see if there's a reaction somewhere in the room, such as a buzz or a light that turns on or off.

MICRODOT PRINTING

Microdot puzzles take advantage of a cool type of printing that makes text super tiny. Like the size of the period at the end of this sentence (hence the name).

While the period in the previous sentence is not an example of microdot printing, you can see that you would have to use a magnifying glass to read it, if it were.

MATH

You're likely to encounter math puzzles in many games, especially in themes like a science laboratory or a classroom. These may be as simple as calculating and filling in the blanks of an equation to get a padlock code.

LIGHT

With light puzzles, information is conveyed through illumination of some kind, sometimes as a light bulb or LED turning on or off, on its own or in response to a player's action.

An example:

As the players move around the room, they notice lights that flash, seemingly for no reason. They eventually realize that their locations in the room correspond to specific lights, and that they need to stand in a pattern to turn on all the lights at once.

SOUND

These puzzles are conveyed through audio narration, music, or other sound clues.

Example:

Narrator: Once upon a time . . .

Soundtrack: [sound of bird calling three times]

Narrator: There was a magical land . . .

Soundtrack: [sound of cat meowing twice]

Narrator: That was full of magical animals.

Soundtrack: [sound of dog barking once]

In this puzzle, the audio of animal noises is giving us information. The bird calling three times, the cat meowing twice, and the dog barking once give us the numbers 3, 2, and 1, which might be used with another puzzle or on a lock in the game.

———

In some escape rooms, several types of codes and puzzles might be combined.

Take this one, for example:

These pieces are all clearly connected, as they are the same shape and have similar patterns. But laid flat on a table, there is no obvious way to connect them and create a solution.

However, when the pieces are assembled into a 3D cube, a clear picture emerges:

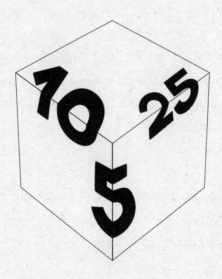

These numbers might translate to letters, or spell out a single number that's part of a larger set required to open a padlock.

Pay attention to the types of puzzles you find in games. With practice, you'll begin to recognize them and eventually will be able to see them behind their concealments.

That's all part of the fun of being a puzzler!

CHAPTER 27

Common Patterns

In this chapter, I've outlined a list of the most common puzzle patterns. Of course, there are many more out there. But if you familiarize yourself with these patterns, you'll be ready to recognize them when they show up in a game.

Always remember that good escape rooms don't require players to bring in outside knowledge. In other words, you don't have to memorize the works of Shakespeare to be able to solve a Shakespeare-themed puzzle inside an escape room game. The room itself should provide all the information you need, in the form of clues or reference materials.

That said, it's never a bad idea to come prepared!

Here are some common sorting and ordering patterns to look out for.

COLOR SPECTRUM

Red

Orange

Yellow

Green

Blue

Indigo

Violet

Or, ROYGBIV. If you see this written out like someone's name ("Roy G. Biv"), it's a good indication that you'll be working with colors.

COLOR WHEEL

The color wheel is often used in puzzles, so get to know color combinations and complementary colors.

The color wheel is: red, blue, yellow.

Color combinations are:

Red + Blue = Purple

Blue + Yellow = Green

Red + Yellow = Orange

And finally, Red + Green = Brown

You might see these as actual colors, but they can also be represented as letters, too.

Keeping that in mind, try to solve this puzzle:

What's something you might find in an escape room?

Red + Blue

Red

Red + Yellow

Red + Blue

A _ _ _ _

HEIGHT OF LIQUID OR OBJECTS

In some puzzles, you're looking for a way to put things into a particular order so that you can decipher a word or figure out the correct way to assemble a set of otherwise random numbers.

One method for ordering a set of objects is by relative size. If you have four bottles that each contain a different amount of liquid, you might try placing them into an order from least amount to greatest amount. A set of wax candles could also be easily assembled in height order, revealing some further piece of information.

If you have a grouping of similar objects whose main difference is height (or size or weight), you're likely looking at this type of puzzle.

SORTING BY WEIGHT

Some puzzles ask you to sort things by weight. If there are scales in the room, this will be obvious, but I've seen them concealed before (for example, one was part of a tabletop), so be on the lookout. You may also be looking at a sorting puzzle when you have a group of objects wherein some are noticeably heavier than others. Of course, this could also be a red herring (see the next chapter on those) so don't let yourself get too distracted by individual heavy or light objects. But if there are scales present, you'll know what to do.

NUMBER OF SIDES
(COULD ALSO BE NUMBER OF POINTS)

If you find yourself with a grouping of similar objects, try counting the sides, or the number of points.

For example, a star has five points, and ten sides. Either of these might reveal a number that becomes part of a needed code.

CARD SUITS

In a deck of fifty-two playing cards, the suit is one of four categories that the cards are divided into. In most traditional decks of cards, the suits are hearts, diamonds, spades, and clubs.

PERIODIC TABLE

The periodic table is also a way that elements like numbers or patterns can be translated into letters.

For example, the numbers 15-1-39-14-55 correspond to phosphorus (P), hydrogen (H), yttrium (Y), silicon (Si), and cesium (Cs). Put together, that spells "PHYSICS."

ZODIAC SYMBOLS

The zodiac refers to parts of the celestial sphere as Earth moves in orbit around the sun. In Western astrology, the zodiac is divided into twelve signs based on constellations, corresponding to segments of a year. In Chinese astrology, the zodiac is divided into a twelve-year repeating cycle, with each year associated with an animal.

OTHER POSSIBLE CUES INCLUDE COUNTRY FLAGS, GREEK LETTERS, OR MUSIC NOTATION

Music notation is another way that symbols can be translated into letters.

C   D   E   F   G   A   B   C

Can you solve this puzzle by figuring out which notes correspond to which letters?

There are many additional ways that information can be encoded.

You can get a hint about what types of codes you might be facing in a room if you find a premade chart or guide.

Don't worry—you won't be expected to memorize any of these beforehand.

MORE PRO TIPS FROM ESCAPE ROOM REVIEWERS

David and Lisa Spira of Room Escape Artist share *even more* helpful tips and tricks for escape room players.

Any advice for taking notes?

Lisa: Don't erase your page or Boogie Boards [an electronic writing tablet often used in escape rooms].

David: It's less and less common to get pen and paper in rooms, but sometimes you still need to remember stuff. Especially older rooms, and those rooms also tend to have lots of padlocks. So what I will do is, I will carry around a padlock and use it as external memory. I'll put the numbers into the lock. That way I can't forget it while people are calling out a lot of numbers.

David: It's reasonably common knowledge at this point to search the room before you really start to hyper-focus on anything. But people don't do that in the second room, if a new space opens up.

Any pro tips to share?

David: When the team stalls out, I'll wait thirty seconds. And after about thirty seconds, I will call out, "If we don't make any progress in the next two minutes, we're going to take a hint!" And we almost always make progress. Once I put the team on that clock, we almost always do.

Calling that out early allows people to go and try their last-minute techniques without feeling undermined. If someone is just about to finish something and you call for a hint without warning, it robs that person of a little moment of victory that they should have gotten. So calling out, "Two minutes!" allows people to finish up.

Thoughts on horror games?

David: When you play horror games, in my not even remotely humble opinion, horror games are best experienced with a split between people who are really scared and people who are really brave.

They're both essential. If everyone is brave, then the game is boring, because the brave people have no one to protect, and that protection allows them to feel the horror empathetically, because they get to experience it through the person that they're helping.

And if you have no brave people, you just have a whole bunch of people who made a mistake.

Lisa: And the game goes nowhere.

Do you have any tips for people who are playing virtual games, as opposed to in-person ones?

David: Yes. The number one tip is, don't play with your friends who live near you, or people you see on a regular basis.

Lisa: Especially if it's your regular escape room team.

David: But if you play with people who live far away, an ocean away, a continent away, people you don't normally get to see, then it feels like a reward.

How would you go about forming a team for a virtual or avatar game?

Lisa: In general for avatar games, they're linear. So a smaller team works just fine, because you're not going to be able to split up and do multiple things at once.

Most games, it doesn't really matter if you're two people in the same home. You can choose to sit side by side, or you choose to log in from different computers. Check based on pricing and the style of game whether you will be happier at one computer or two computers. And wear headphones.

Do you have special tips for teams playing virtual games?

David: Start by having a conversation with your teammates about how they want to handle the game. Do you want to take turns giving instructions? Do you have someone on your team who is especially witty and funny? Is it going to be better if they're the one who's calling stuff out because they will be added entertainment?

Lisa: Be mindful of what people want out of the game. Especially in the purely avatar-based games where things are really bottlenecked around how many things the avatar is capable of doing at once—which is usually just one thing at a time.

And for avatar games, understand that the avatar is a player on your team. They're a part of your experience and you can't ignore them. You will have more fun if you interact with them and just engage with them as whatever character they're playing.

How do you approach scheduling online games?

Lisa: Remember time zones. They're hard, but important.

David: For Americans, don't use standard or daylight savings, don't list something as EST or EDT, just say Eastern time or New York time.

Lisa: When I choose games, I note which city the company is in, so that our remote players can choose if they can play that game or if they're going to be in a time zone conundrum. It can get complicated.

CHAPTER 28

Red Herrings

A red herring is a misleading prop or piece of information. These are things that seem relevant but are actually extraneous.

The phrase originated with foxhunting. Trainers would use a fish to lay a trail that dogs would follow. Horses would follow the dogs, and in this way become used to the noise and action that would come during an actual hunt.

But its use to mean a distraction or false clue comes from an 1807 tale by radical journalist William Cobbett, who wrote in the *Weekly Political Register* about how the press sometimes missed important news: "It was a mere transitory effect of the political red-herring; for, on the Saturday, the scent became as cold as a stone."[1]

In escape rooms, the map is blank when you enter. When anything could be a clue or a prop, it's very easy to get distracted. It's also easy to assume that a puzzle is way more complicated than it actually is.

There's a cognitive phenomenon known as "pareidolia," which is the human tendency to detect patterns and faces where there are none.

Have you ever seen a shape in a cloud, or thought a knot in a tree looked like a grumpy old man?

That's pareidolia in action, and it's something we have to be aware of, and guard against, when playing puzzle games.

Remember, the room is not trying to trick you. Clues or puzzles might be hidden, but if you've been warned to not take apart furniture, you can safely disregard that chair, no matter how tempting it may be to unscrew its parts.

Sometimes, designers have accidentally included items for decoration that might make you think they're part of a puzzle. If you notice you've been spending a lot of time trying to make something work with no progress, the answer could be as simple as: it's just a prop.

When in doubt, ask your game monitor.

CHAPTER 29

A Game Monitor's Point of View

I want to talk a bit about what it's like to watch people play a game, as a designer and person who has monitored hundreds of games.

Number one, I want people to win!

I quietly rejoice when someone gets a solve, and even though I can't show it, I am just as excited when something finally opens after someone's spent a lot of time working on it.

Here's the stuff I wish I could say out loud to people:

THE GM IS ROOTING FOR YOU, NOT JUDGING YOU

A lot of people feel hesitant about asking for help because they feel pressured by the need to perform or are afraid of being judged.

This is a totally human response, so I want to reassure you that whoever is watching you play your game is on your side. Please don't be afraid to ask for guidance or a nudge if you need it. (See chapter 22 on how hints work for some tips on ways to phrase these questions.)

YOU'RE PROBABLY CLOSER TO SOLVING IT THAN YOU THINK

Many, *many* times, I've watched somebody get within one or two steps of solving a puzzle, then get frustrated and walk away from it.

In these cases, I wish they would either ask for a nudge or check in with a teammate to see if they have any insight to offer. Sometimes, getting a fresh pair of eyes on it will reveal the answer immediately.

LISTEN TO THE QUIET ONES IN YOUR GROUP

When I'm monitoring a game, I'm listening to everything that every team member says.

Sometimes, a game will have a director (see chapter 15, "Which Type of Escape Room Player Are You?"). This person takes charge of the game, telling people what to solve and how to solve it. The problem is, a lot of the time, they're wrong! But their bossy attitude doesn't leave room for other people to try anything.

When this happens, I often hear a quiet voice speaking up with the right answer. It's the quiet one in the group, someone who's too nervous to make themselves heard, but who does, in fact, know the answer.

So my tip is, listen to the quiet ones in your group.

Whether or not you're in a group with a director, pay attention to what folks are saying. If someone is extra shy, make sure you support them when they speak up.

It's always a good idea to listen to a team member and amplify what they've said, and that is doubly true when it's someone who's on the quieter side.

YOUR FIRST INSTINCT IS PROBABLY PRETTY CLOSE

In other words, don't overthink it. The game is designed to be solved, so your first guess is probably right a lot of the time.

I've seen a lot of people try the correct method but not land on the answer immediately. Especially with mechanical puzzles, like a padlock failing to open because the answer is slightly out of alignment.

Instead of trying again, they dismiss the *method* rather than the incorrect answer and go off on a different path that takes them very far away from the solve.

RELATED: DON'T DISMISS SOMEONE ELSE'S IDEA

If someone has a guess about how to approach a solve, give it a try, even if you think there's no way it will work.

Even trying something wrong will give you information: now you know that the method isn't the right one! Without trying, you can't actually rule it out.

And hey, honestly? A lot of the time, it turns out to be the right method after all.

ASK FOR HELP

We've covered this a lot in the chapter about asking for hints, but I promise, you're going to have more fun if you ask for help when you get stuck.

LOOK AGAIN

Is a puzzle just not solving? Check again: What information do you currently have? What hasn't been used yet? What sort of information do you still need? Sometimes all it takes is looking again at the info, pictures, or room to nudge that final insight into place.

SWAP PLACES AND PUZZLES; GET A PAIR OF FRESH EYES

If you really can't get a solve, pull in a teammate. You can ask them to help you on it, or hand it off completely. Getting a second pair of eyes or hands on a puzzle that seems stuck is a great way to unstick it—plus it's more fun to solve with friends.

PLEASE DON'T CLIMB ON THAT/TOUCH THAT/ PUT YOUR FINGER IN THAT

This applies to in-person games, so bear it in mind. I don't want to have to interrupt your game and say something about safety, because it distracts you from the puzzles and breaks your fantasy of immersion. So do us all a solid and don't do something that requires me to step in before you injure yourself.

CHAPTER 30

Technology and Electronics

Clarke's third law:
Any sufficiently advanced technology is indistinguishable from magic.

In-person and online escape rooms can vary in the amount of technology that they utilize for communication, puzzles, and props.

Some rooms have only "mechanical" puzzles. That is to say, the puzzles are all physical objects and interacting with them doesn't automatically trigger something (like a drawer popping open), though it may progress you through the room.

Some rooms are stuffed full of electronic props and sensors. These games are more likely to have interactive or magical-seeming puzzles.

Many rooms fall somewhere in between.

The electronics used in building games are generally repeated over different rooms, and recognizing how these electronics work will help you understand how to interact with the objects you might find in a game.

This is a form of "back-solving": looking at the end goal to determine what steps you need to take to reach it.

PROXIMITY SENSORS AND RFID

You touch the tip of a magic wand to a word in a book, and a lantern suddenly lights up. You place a carved figure on a shelf, and you hear the click of a drawer unlocking. These are puzzles that utilize sensors to recognize the placement of an item.

Often to progress the player must touch objects in a specific order, or arrange the objects in a specific way, to trigger the sensors.

You can sometimes recognize these because there will be a designated space to insert the item, such as an indentation in a surface.

ELECTROMAGNETS

You successfully enter a secret code, and a brick falls open in front of your eyes: it's actually a secret compartment on a hinge, and it has a key inside.

Remember how "there are only so many ways to lock a box"?

An alternative is to use electromagnets. These are pieces of metal that, when an electrical current is run through them, become magnetic. These are aligned with a metal plate. When the current is stopped, the magnet releases.

This is a great way to "magically" close things and to introduce an element of surprise when they are unlocked.

They will usually be concealed in some way, since they can become hot to the touch after a while. You can also sometimes spot them because there may be wires or a conduit leading to the magnetized object from the wall.

As you continue to play escape rooms, you will become very familiar with the *click* these make when they release.

CHAPTER 31

Playing at Home

If you're planning to play escape room games at home, whether that's a board game, video game, or one that takes another form, you will still find the tips in this book to be very helpful.

The principles of teamwork, communication, clues, and puzzles are universal, no matter what environment you're in or what type of game you're playing.

There are lots of virtual experiences and games designed to play at home. Try some out—you just might discover a new hobby.

FIGURING OUT YOUR SETUP

Before you play a game at home, whether it's online or at a table, you should spend some time beforehand thinking about your physical setup.

If you're playing a game on the computer, do you have a comfortable chair? Are your headphones charged? Do you have a pencil and paper at hand, ready to use?

If you're at a table, is there adequate lighting? Do you have some water nearby?

Before playing a computer-based game with another person in your same household, decide if you'll share one screen or use separate computers. It can take a while to figure out the right microphone and head-phone configuration, and you and your team will have a lot more fun if they don't have to wait for you.

AVATAR AND HOSTED VIRTUAL GAMES

This style of virtual escape room is a first-person experience that you play through the Internet. We discussed these in an earlier chapter of this book, but there are a few more tips that will make your experience even better.

First, pick who will relay information to the avatar. If you have a funny or charming member of your team, this can be a great role, since they can ham it up and it will add to the group's fun.

Second, consider the avatar to be a member of your team. I've heard about teams who will totally mute themselves, or who will speak on a different voice channel so that the avatar can't hear them.

This is just like cutting out a member of your team—this person is there to help you, and they need to know what you're thinking about the various puzzles if they're going to give you good hints!

And finally, see if your team might be interested in dressing up in costumes for the occasion. It can make for a very fun team picture after you're done.

UNHOSTED GAME

For an unhosted game, it's a good idea to check all the aforementioned things regarding your tech setup and whether you'll be comfortable. It's also wise to note whether the game offers a hint system, or if there's a customer service email or number you can call in case you get stuck on something.

BOARD GAMES

Settling in for a board game night? Here are some things to keep in mind.

Setting the Scene

Think about the ambiance of your game. You can use lighting, music, scents, and even food to help bring a little bit of the fictional world to life.

Playing a sci-fi themed game set on a spaceship? Pull up the soundtrack to your favorite cyborgs-in-space show and turn on some neon-colored lights.

If you're tackling a detective game set in the 1800s, candles and classical music might set the right tone.

Costumes and accessories can also be a lot of fun—just make sure it's something you're comfortable sitting down in, and that your accessories won't get in the way of gameplay. It's probably pretty tough to shuffle cards with silky gloves on, but a sparkly ring would catch that candlelight very nicely.

Game Setup

Before playing a board game with a lot of complicated parts and rules, one person should check out everything in advance, as the game might require some setup or special arrangement.

Some games require downloading an app, or putting together pieces for the board. Some board games even include battery-operated parts! And some games might require special tools like blacklights.

Whatever the case, it's best to discover these needs early so that they can be taken care of before game night is supposed to begin.

A note on spoilers: there is a very small possibility that the person doing setup might encounter spoilers for the rest of the game. With most commercial games, you won't have to worry about this at all. But for some smaller or indie games, it's a possibility, so let's talk about it.

For example, something might need assembly; the person doing the assembling would therefore need to know about a hidden passageway in a dollhouse, in order to construct around it.

Generally, people posting on game forums are pretty good about labeling spoilers in comments, so if you post your own comment, please be sure to extend the same courtesy to other readers.

THE NEXT LEVEL

So let's say you've played every commercial and indie escape room game out there. (Congrats, and go you!) Are there more puzzles to be had?

The good news is, yes! There is a thriving community of puzzle makers who offer their stuff online. They offer different difficulty levels, but are generally on the side of "more advanced."

A good place to start is Puzzled Pint. Every month since 2010, they've created and shared a unique set of puzzles, which are available to download for free at puzzledpint.com.

CHAPTER 32

Making Games Yourself

So, you've read all about escape rooms, and maybe even played a few. Now you want to make one yourself—hooray!

Before we begin, it has to be said that designing, building, and opening a physical escape room space to run as a business is a huge endeavor. It involves permits, leases, construction, and a whole lot of time and money put into running a small business. It's a full-time job, and then some.

Yes, the game design is very fun, but that part ends quickly. If you're not interested in running a ticket-selling business, I'd recommend sticking to the DIY versions that we'll discuss here.

Designing a puzzle game for friends, family, or even strangers can be very fun and creatively fulfilling.

Making puzzles is also a good way to get better at solving them—after all, once you understand what goes into a puzzle, and how information is transformed or concealed, your method of thinking and approaching puzzles on the other side is bound to improve. Plus, you will learn a lot about what to do and what to avoid when you see people struggle or successfully solve a puzzle.

So, if you want to make a game, here are some questions to go over before you get started:

FIRST, ASK YOURSELF: WHO AM I MAKING THIS FOR?

I'd recommend starting out with a game for family or friends. It's also going to be easier to make a game for a few people at a time, rather than many.

Your end goal will be to create a game that is fun and keeps everyone occupied the whole time. The more people who are solving, the more puzzles you'll need.

THEN, THINK ABOUT SCALE

Is this a game for a friend's birthday party that you'll run over a video call, or will you create something for your family to play all day on a Saturday in your backyard?

My tip is to keep it simple—it's easy to make things more complicated if needed, but it's a lot harder to simplify something that starts out with a lot of moving parts.

IS THERE A TIME LIMIT?

An all-day-long scavenger hunt is going to be pretty different from a thirty-minute timed challenge, so think about what time constraints you want to place on the game. If you're not sure, start with an hour and see how it goes. You can always change a part later if it turns out people will need more time to complete it.

THEN, THE BIG ONES: WHAT IS YOUR STORY? AND WHAT ARE YOU GOING TO ASK PLAYERS TO DO?

One way to come up with a story idea is to think about the setting first, whether you're making an in-person game or a digital one. If it's in your backyard, has the area become suddenly magical, or taken over by aliens? If you're making an online game, are you trying to learn the secrets of a candy factory, or complete a school assignment?

Whatever your setting, think about stories taking place there that you would find fun or interesting. Also consider what the players' final goal is going to be. A candy lab might be about discovering a secret formula for a new concoction, while a school classroom could conceal a message hidden in an ancient book.

Then, think about the tone. Do you want your game to be funny, thrilling, or scary? That school classroom could be about a hidden world of wizards, or the site of a secret spy-training program. A candy factory could be jolly and colorful, or run-down and sinister.

NEXT, COME UP WITH SOME IDEAS FOR PUZZLES THAT MAKE SENSE IN THAT SETTING

If your final goal is discovering a secret candy formula for the most awesome chocolate bar that ever existed, you're probably going to do some chemistry, shuffle around some papers, and maybe eat some sweets along the way. Candy is colorful and comes in a lot of shapes. And a factory has a lot of textures: liquid, sticky, gooey.

There are so many possibilities! Look at the chapter on types of puzzles and think of ways you might adapt them to your theme. For example, invisible ink could be used on the inside of a candy wrapper, and different colors and shapes of candy could be used to form a code, spelling out a word.

You can also combine puzzles to make them more complicated, and add steps to a puzzle. For example, you might first ask people to assemble a picture. The picture might then contain a blacklight message that's only legible after being assembled.

CREATING YOUR FIRST PUZZLE

For your first game, you should aim for most puzzles to be solvable in five to ten minutes. This helps you do two things: one, you can make sure your puzzles are the right difficulty. Two, you can figure out how many puzzles you need to create.

It is very likely that the first puzzles you make will be *way* too hard or *way* too simple. That's okay! You will learn by doing. And the best way to learn these lessons is through playtesting.

PLAYTESTING

Playtesting is the process of giving your puzzles to people who have never seen them before so that you can watch as they attempt to solve them.

It's a very important part of design, because it reveals a puzzle's strengths and weaknesses before it's in the hands of the intended audience. So if you can, have a friend or two play your game before you finalize it.

Seeing people try to solve something will tell you valuable information about your puzzle. Watch them carefully, but don't give them any hints. It's especially important to let them *fail* to solve it, because this tells you which parts are hard to understand, or aren't working.

Through this method, you can learn what adjustments the puzzle will need so that people can solve it successfully.

It can be hard to watch people struggle, especially because it will seem so obvious to you, the designer. But if you just give in and tell them the answer, you'll never learn the valuable information of what to adjust to create the best version of the puzzle.

It's also important to learn to set aside your ego. It's hard when you spend a lot of time designing something, and you feel very clever and proud of yourself, and then it just isn't working. It's even harder when you make adjustments, and something about it still isn't right.

But you want the game to be the best it possibly can be, right? (Right.) So put that puzzle into a folder and save it for another time. Often when you revisit, the flaws become clear—and fixable.

PUZZLE PRESENTATION

Think about how you'll present the puzzles to the players. Will they be objects around a room, or a series of locked boxes with padlocks? Do you want to bury something in your garden? Will people be uncovering a series of password-protected websites? Have you mailed a small box of surprises to people to be opened only when the game begins?

Think back on your theme, and try to tie it to every puzzle.

You'll also have to decide how to "gate" the puzzles. "Gating" is the method for blocking access to puzzles that should only be available later in the game.

In other words, how are you going to keep someone from solving a puzzle too quickly, or skipping ahead to a later one?

If the puzzles are all out at once, players might not know where to start solving them. Or they could grab the second-to-last puzzle, figure out its answer, and be done with the game almost immediately. By gating puzzles, you control the order in which people are able to play the game. To determine your gating strategy, you should think about the overall structure of the game, and work backward from the end goal.

Let's say that the player's final goal, the thing that ends the game and lets them win, is to discover the secret formula for a new candy bar, and the last task people perform is to "create" that candy bar, which they can then eat. Sounds great!

What are the steps that get them to that end goal?

Well, first they might have to figure out someone's email password so that they can hack into the candy company's computer system. The puzzles are gated because there's a password to get into the next part, and nothing else is solvable until that is done.

Then, after doing some corporate espionage, they might have to collect flowers and herbs to create parts of the secret formula. If the secret formula must be input into a machine before it produces the final candy bar, this step is gated off because no matter what the players try to do, the machine won't operate without the right combination.

And so on. As you playtest, you will want to keep an eye out for places where people can potentially skip steps. Sometimes fixing that is as simple as putting something into a locked box or behind a password-protected website.

PUZZLE FLOW

In a puzzle game, you want people to be able to have fun. Sometimes, the best situation is if they totally forget they're playing a game because they're so wrapped up in it.

To do this, you want to make sure that nothing is so hard or distracting that it takes them out of the moment. A puzzle being too difficult, or players being confused about what the next step is in the game, takes them out of their immersion in the story.

So as you design, remember that each puzzle should somehow lead to the next one.

The simplest way to do this for a homemade game is for the players to tell you the correct answer, and you hand them the next puzzle or give them the next link or image. The slightly more complex way is for the answer from one puzzle to connect to the next one.

Let's dig into that a bit more.

In the candy factory, maybe your players have to unwrap a bunch of candy bars. They might discover that the patterns on the wrappers form one big picture. When they flip that picture over, they might find a message: "Squeeze the Twinkies."

That tells them that their next step is—you might have guessed this—to squeeze the Twinkies.

But if the Twinkies were just sitting out on a table, they might have already squeezed them, skipping the wrapper puzzle entirely. So you need to gate the Twinkies. Let's say you put them into a safe with a combination lock.

Now you need to give the players the combination to that lock. If you put it on the wrappers along with the "Squeeze" message, you guarantee that they won't solve it out of order.

A BIG FINISH

Once you have your puzzles outlined, think about the ending again.

You have your final goal: figure out the most amazing secret candy formula. But what happens when the players reach that goal? You want to be sure that the ending is satisfying.

Another important thing is that it should feel like the players really earned it.

This is the reason why so many older escape rooms ended with finding a key that opened the final door. There's something very satisfying about knowing what you're looking for (the key), finding it, and getting a response from the game (the door opening).

Maybe in your game, the secret candy formula is actually rocket fuel, so they push a big red button that sends a rocket ship flying. (This can be a paper rocket ship on a string. What matters is that there's a reaction to their action.)

That sounds really fun! But you know what would make it even better? If the rocket ship has actual candy inside it that the players get to eat when they've won.

———————

Again, it's a very good idea to have someone, or more than one someone, test the game.

There's a thin line between "fun challenge" and "frustration," and you want to make sure you're staying on the right side of it. The way to do that is to make sure that all the wrinkles get ironed out before you put it in front of your players.

Practice makes perfect. Play as many games as you can to learn what makes a puzzle good or bad, and create lots of test versions of your own puzzles until you start to get the hang of it.

With all these tips, you should be able to create a fun game for your friends or family.

And with the tips in the rest of the book, you should be armed with the skills and knowledge to be successful in any escape room that you decide to tackle.

Good luck, player!

GLOSSARY

5 Wits

A chain of entertainment venues in the northeastern United States, featuring interactive adventure games. Opened in 2004.

AD&D

(*See: Dungeons & Dragons*)

affordance

A property of an object that shows a user how it can be used or interacted with.

"Aha!" moment

The moment when suddenly a concept or solution clicks into place, and you understand what you're supposed to do next.

Alberti disk

A cipher method written about by Leon Battista Alberti in 1467. There are two disks, one large and one small. The outer disk is fixed, and contains the alphabet and numbers 1–4. The inner disk rotates and contains the alphabet. Spinning the inner disk to match a letter on the outer disk provides a polyalphabetic substitution.

alternate reality game (ARG)

"Alternate reality game" is the term used for an interactive story that combines the real world and digital or media sources. (*See also: The Beast, transmedia*)

Arcade

A venue containing games, video game cabinets, pinball machines, and other amusements. Originally known as "penny arcades" in the early 1900s, which contained mechanical coin-operated devices, the introduction of video games in the late 1970s led to an increase in the eighties of "video arcades."

Bauta mask

A character from the annual Carnival of Venice festival held in Italy, leading up to Lent. The Bauta is a full-face mask with a prominent nose, no mouth, and a large chin.

The Beast

The first alternate reality game (*see entry*). Developed in 2001 by Microsoft to promote the film *A.I. Artificial Intelligence* and set about forty years after the events of the film.

The Blair Witch Project

An early example of transmedia (*see entry*).

board game

A form of tabletop game. These use a flat board and pieces that are moved according to a set of rules.

book cipher

A cipher that utilizes a book or piece of text as its decryption key.

braille

A writing system created by Louis Braille in 1824 for people who are visually impaired. It is tactile and uses a raised texture on paper.

brute-forcing

A time-consuming method for solving puzzles. Solvers systematically try every possible option until they hit the correct solution.

Burning Man

An annual event held in a temporary city in the Black Rock Desert of northwest Nevada since 1986. It is an experimental festival that uses a barter system and practices the principle of "leave no trace."

Burr puzzle

An interlocking puzzle that combines notched pieces to form a 3D object.

Caesar cipher; shift cipher

A substitution cipher named for Julius Caesar. Each letter in the unencrypted alphabet is replaced by a letter a fixed number of positions down.

Cloudmakers

The community of people that formed around the first alternate reality game (*see entry*), The Beast (*see entry*).

clue

A piece of evidence or information used to solve a mystery. In escape rooms, it may be a piece of information found inside the game, or a hint (*see entry*) given to the player to help them along.

confirmation; verification

When a player thinks they have a code right but can't enter it correctly into a padlock or other vehicle, they can ask for a confirmation to see if the problem lies with the code or the mechanism.

Crimson Room

An early digital point-and-click adventure game created by Toshi-mitsu Takagi in 2004. Games of this genre are sometimes known as Takagism.

cryptex

A type of lockbox consisting of a cylinder surrounded by letter wheels. The word was created for the book *The Da Vinci Code* by Dan Brown and is a portmanteau of the Greek word κρυπτός, *kryptós*, meaning "hidden" or "secret," and the Latin word *caudex*, meaning "trunk of a tree" or "block of wood."

The Crystal Maze

A British game show set in a large space with four themed zones. Contestant teams must undertake a variety of timed challenges, including physical and mental, to earn crystals.

Dungeons & Dragons (D&D, AD&D)

A tabletop role-playing game created in the 1970s by war gamers Gary Gygax and Dave Arneson. Played with a group of people, it is an exercise in collaborative storytelling led by a dungeon master, or DM.

electromagnet; maglock

A lock consisting of two metal plates that become magnetic when an electrical current is run through them.

embodied

To express in concrete form. In the context of virtual reality and immersive entertainment, embodiment refers to the awareness of being in a temporal moment, within a human body, usually in a physical space.

Glossary

experiential entertainment

An amusement, performance, or other type of entertainment that is centered around something a person experiences directly, as opposed to something a person experiences through a screen.

fair; festival

A fair or festival is an in-person gathering for trade, commerce, art, music, performance, community, or all of the above.

flash mob

An entertainment event when a group of people suddenly assemble in a public space, perform an action like a dance or applauding, and quickly disperse.

flow state

Being "in the zone." A form of deep concentration where a person is focused, immersed, and enjoying their activity. Named by Mihaly Csikszentmihalyi in 1975.

fourth wall

A term from theater and performance. If a stage has three physical walls, there is also an invisible wall that separates the actors from the audience. The actors typically behave as if they cannot see through the wall, while the audience can. In some theatrical performances, the actors interact directly with the audience; this is known as "breaking the fourth wall."

frame; framing device

The frame or framing device of a story is the narrative reason for the player or viewer to be present. For example, they may have been invited by a relative, or be a guest of a hotel.

free party

A British movement of the 1970s–1990s, free parties were counter-cultural events thrown by and for people gathering to listen to music and celebrate art, often in the countryside.

game master (GM); dungeon master (DM)

A term from tabletop role-playing games. A person who oversees gameplay, enforces rules, and moderates the environment. For Dungeons & Dragons (*see entry*), the game master is the dungeon master (DM).

gorilla experiment

A form of perceptual blindness, when a person fails to notice or see something fully visible due to the amount of stimulus in the scene. Coined by Arien Mack and Irvin Rock in 1992.

hieroglyphics

The writing system used in ancient Egypt.

hint; hint system

In a puzzle game, a hint is a way to nudge a player onto the right path to solving a puzzle. A hint system is the mechanism for delivering that hint and may come via a digital screen, a paper note, a walkie-talkie, or a human voice.

human circuit puzzle

A human circuit puzzle uses human bodies to conduct a low-voltage electrical current from one conductive pad to another.

Imagineering

A combination of the words "imagination" and "engineering," used to describe the practical creation of innovative ideas, especially at Disney theme parks.

immersive

    A term referring to art and experiences characterized by deep absorption or the suspension of disbelief.

indexing

    The technique of extracting a letter from a word, based on information given in the puzzle in sets of numbers and letters.

leap of logic

    A leap of logic in a puzzle game is a surprising step, or one that is not well explained, requiring people to make their best guess at a solution.

Legends of the Hidden Temple

    An American action-adventure children's game show from the early 1990s.

Lost Vagueness

    A Carnivalesque event held at the Glastonbury Festival in England from 2000 to 2007, with roots in the free-party movement.

maze

    A system of paths and barriers that a player must find their way through.

metapuzzle; meta

    A compound puzzle, solved by completing earlier puzzles in a game or set.

midway

    A place or avenue at a circus or fair with a concentration of games, booths, and rides.

MIT Mystery Hunt

A weekend-long puzzle game that began on the campus of the Massachusetts Institute of Technology in Boston, Massachusetts, in 1981.

Morse code

A method of encoding text characters using dots and dashes, named for telegraph inventor Samuel Morse.

number pad

Number pads are rectangular grids of numbers, like a touch pad you would use to enter a restricted building or digits found on a telephone.

Olympics; Olympic Games

An ancient festival held in Olympia, Greece, to showcase athleticism and culture, and a modern revival of the event that celebrates international unity through sports.

ordering

Ordering is using any information that tells you what order to place individual puzzle components, so that you can read them correctly as or after you solve them.

padlock

A lock with a shackle that is passed through an opening and secured in itself.

ParaPark

One of the first formal escape rooms in the world. Founded by Attila Gyurkovics in 2011.

pigpen cipher

A symbol-based substitution cipher. Letters are replaced by fragments of a grid upon which they are placed.

play

Activities done for pleasure and enjoyment.

Pong

A digital game of table tennis, featuring two vertical lines representing paddles and a dot representing a ball. One of the first-ever arcade games, released in 1972, and one of the first-ever video games, released in 1975.

postal game; play-by-mail game; PBM game

Any game played through postal mail or email, such as correspondence chess.

presence

In virtual reality, presence is the suspension of disbelief and awareness of a new self that occurs, allowing the user to feel as if they are actually inhabiting a virtual environment

promenade theater; site-specific theater

A theatrical production designed around a specific, nontheater location, or one in which the actors or audience members move around the space.

prop

An object found inside an escape room that may contain a puzzle, tell something about the story of the game, or be purely decorative.

proscenium arch

The frame around a stage, and the space between the curtain and the orchestra. It serves as a way to define the action on the stage and forms an invisible wall between the audience and the actors. (*See also: fourth wall*)

puzzle

A game, question, or challenge that tests a person's ingenuity or knowledge.

puzzle hunt

A game where teams compete to solve a series of puzzles. Puzzle hunts can be confined to one location or take place across multiple sites. (*See also: MIT Mystery Hunt, Puzzled Pint*)

Puzzled Pint

A monthly puzzle-solving event, founded in Portland, Oregon, in 2010. Free archives available at http://puzzledpint.com.

rabbit hole

A reference to *Alice in Wonderland*, denoting the moment that a new player stumbles upon an entry point into an alternate reality game's story, puzzles, or world.

red herring

Anything that misleads a player. It could be a deliberate diversion, such as an extra-challenging puzzle that leads to dead ends, or an accidental distraction, such as when decor appears to be part of a puzzle but is actually irrelevant.

reset

After a group leaves an escape room game, the staff will put all the puzzles, props, and other items into their default place so that the next group can experience the room.

RFID

Stands for "radio-frequency identification." The use of electro-magnetic fields to detect objects with RFID tags.

riddle

A deliberately mystifying question, to be solved or guessed as part of a game.

safe; lockout safe

A secure cabinet with a strong lock. Some safes with digital number pads will temporarily "lock out" a user after a number of incorrect guesses of its password.

scavenger hunt

A game in which people on teams hunt for items on a list provided by organizers.

SCRAP

A puzzle event company founded in Kyoto, Japan, in 2007 by Takao Kato. SCRAP brought the first formal escape rooms to the United States in 2012.

scytale

A tool used to create a transposition cipher. A long, thin strip of paper, parchment, or leather is wrapped around a cylinder, so that its letters align in readable rows.

semaphore

A naval system of communication utilizing flags in various arm positions, which may be seen at a distance.

signifier

An element of design that suggests or describes how an item might be interacted with.

site-specific theater; environmental theater

A type of theatrical production performed in a unique location and designed to be responsive to that location.

Sleep No More

A production of Shakespeare's *Macbeth* set in a 1940s noir hotel, created by London immersive design group Punchdrunk.

soundalike

A word or phrase that can be spoken aloud to decipher what words match to it phonetically.

Suicide Club; Cacophony Society

A California-based performance and prank group.

suspension of disbelief

An intentional state of mind in which a person willingly avoids examining a situation or story in a way that would break the illusion that it is real.

tabletop game

A board game, role-playing game, or any other type of game that is played on a large, flat surface like a table.

Glossary

Takagism

A term for digital point-and-click adventure games, named for the creator of Crimson Room (2004), Toshimitsu Takagi. (*See also: Crimson Room*)

tangram

A dissection puzzle with flat shapes that fit together, as a puzzle, inside of a square or other silhouette.

team building

An activity or process that directs a group of people to work together as a team on collaborative and cooperative tasks.

theme park

An amusement park with rides and games, with a central theme uniting its structures and attractions.

transmedia

Telling a single story, or telling stories set in the same world, across multiple digital platforms.

trolley parks

Recreation areas created at the end of streetcar lines, featuring picnic areas and concert pavilions.

virtual reality (VR)

Computer-generated simulations of 3D environments, scenes, or activities. Users can inhabit or interact with these scenes through the use of electronic headsets.

walkthrough

A post-game experience in which a game master takes the players through the game they have just completed, to show them the puzzles and story elements in order.

war game

A type of tabletop game built around a map or strategic area, and utilizing painted miniature figures.

zine; fanzine

Short for "magazine." A self-published printed work, usually created for a small group of people. A popular way to distribute fan fiction, subculture news, comics, and other text and image-based material within a community.

RECOMMENDED READING

If you are interested in the design and philosophy of immersive and interactive work, these are excellent resources for education.

A Theory of Fun for Game Design by Raph Koster (2004).

The Art of Immersion: How the Digital Generation Is Remaking Hollywood, Madison Avenue, and the Way We Tell Stories by Frank Rose (2011).

Hamlet on the Holodeck: The Future of Narrative in Cyberspace by Janet H. Murray (2016).

Nordic Larp by Jaakko Stenros and Markus Montola (2010).

Odyssey Works: Transformative Experiences for an Audience of One by Abraham Burickson and Ayden LeRoux (2016) .

The Punchdrunk Encyclopaedia by Josephine Machon (2018).

Puzzlecraft: How to Make Every Kind of Puzzle by Mike Selinker and Thomas Snyder (2013).

Theme Park Design & The Art of Themed Entertainment by Joe Rohde (2016).

WEBSITES

ARGNet: Alternate Reality Gaming Network, http://argn.com.

No Proscenium: The Guide to Everything Immersive, http://noproscenium .com.

Room Escape Artist, http://roomescapeartist.com.

SOLUTIONS

EDGAR ALLAN POE CIPHER

Poe published the solution to this cipher in the October 1841 issue of *Graham's Magazine*. The answer is: "This specimen of secret writing is sent you for explanation. If you succeed in divining its meaning, I will believe that you are some kin to Old Nick."

LETTER-FINDING

The answer to this puzzle is found by writing out the underlined letters in the sentence. The answer is: ROSE

ALPHANUMERIC

Using the chart of letters that correspond to numbers, the answer is: MARBLE

MORSE CODE

The beads on the necklace correspond to Morse letters. The answer is: PEARL

BINARY

The seahorses and starfish correspond to 1s (seahorses) and 0s (starfish), making binary letters. The answer is: SEA

INDEXING

Index the number into the ingredient only, not the amount of the ingredient. For example, the fourth letter of sugar is A. This gives the answer: CAKE

ACROSTIC

Reading the first letter of each sentence gives the answer: GEORGIANA

BOOK CIPHER

Looking at the chapter, paragraph, and word indicated by each set of numbers, the answer is: WELL DONE READER AND THANK YOU

SEMAPHORE

The leaves of the flowers form semaphore letters. The answer is: BLOOM

PIGPEN

The shapes correspond to letters of the alphabet. The answer is THATS ALL FOLKS

Solutions

NATO

The words "Bravo," "Oscar," and "Kilo" correspond to letters in the NATO alphabet. Read together in the sentence, they spell out: BOOK

DROP-DOWN LETTERS

Each word in this sequence changes one letter from the previous word. The answers are:

HARD

CARD

CART

CAST

EAST

EASY

REBUS

The rebus spells out: BEAUTY IS IN THE EYE OF THE BEHOLDER

ALIGNMENT

Looking at the text from the edge of the book, the answer is: NOW YOU SEE ME

NUMBER PAD

Each number has dots underneath it. These dots correspond to a letter on the number pad. So three dots under the number 2 means to use the third letter on the 2 on the number pad, for example. The answer is: CONNECTION

NONOGRAM

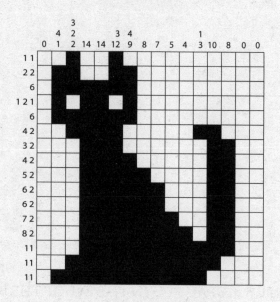

COLOR WHEEL

Combining the colors gives you "Purple," "Red," "Orange," and "Purple." Taking the first letter of each color gives the answer: PROP

MUSIC NOTATION

The answer is: CABBAGE

ACKNOWLEDGMENTS

Thank you to all of the people who generously allowed me to interview them for this book for the gift of your time and insights.

Thanks to the community of escape room players, makers, and enthusiasts for making the hobby so enjoyable.

Thank you to Emily Carleton, Samantha Lubash, Natasha Yglesias, Michael Anderson, and the whole Tiller Press crew for your wonderful support and guidance. Thanks also to cover designer Patrick Sullivan, designer Davina Mock, copy editor Erica Ferguson, managing editor Annie Craig, marketers Laura Flavin, Molly Pieper, and Kayla Bartee, production editor Laura Jarrett, production manager Allison Har-zvi, and publicists Lauren Ollerhead and Nan Rittenhouse.

Extra-special thanks to Beth Wilbins for your careful reading and thoughtful advice. I love you!

Thank you to Ricky Haggett for your wisdom and encouragement.

Thanks to Risa Puno for your support and perspective.

Thanks to Kathryn Yu and Noah Nelson of No Proscenium and Lisa and David Spira of Room Escape Artist for all the work they do on behalf of the immersive and escape room communities.

Extra thanks to Kathryn for our long conversations and for helping me confirm some small but important details.

Thanks to my original puzzle-solving team and fellow Spark of Resistance makers, Dave Aldhouse, Matt Cleinman, Mink ette, and Victor Asteinza. I wouldn't be here without you.

Thanks to my Meridian Adventure Co. crew, who are making magic

Acknowledgments

real: KL Cullom, Foley, Travis McClanahan, Jessica Lachenal, Jerry Belich, David Dowling, and the many others who have contributed their time, talent, and expertise to our projects.

Thank you to Nora Ryan for keeping the plates spinning and making all of this possible.

Thank you to the Every Game in this City crew for your conversation and company, which has made a long, difficult lockdown year a lot easier: Alexandra Lee, Amani Naseem, Chad Toprak, Douglas Wilson, Goldie Bartlett, Lee Shang Lun, Melissa McGlensey, Patrick LeMieux, and Stephanie Boluk.

Thanks to my family. Our weekly Zoom calls and holiday celebrations have been a balm.

Thanks to all my friends who love games, puzzles, stories, and mysteries, and especially giving those things as gifts to others through their own work.

Thank you to everyone who's supported this book, chatted with me on Twitter, and shared their excitement about escape rooms with me.

And above all, thank you to my partner, Jey Biddulph, who's always on my team.

CHAPTER 2: ANCIENT HISTORY TO THE 1800S

1. *Waverly Free Press*, March 23, 1889.
2. *Waverly Free Press*, November 23, 1889.
3. John Horne and Garry Whannel, *Understanding the Olympics* (Abingdon, UK: Routledge, 2012).
4. Philip Barker, *The Story of the Olympic Torch* (Stroud, UK: Amberley, 2012).
5. Peter Burke, *Popular Culture in Early Modern Europe* (Aldershot, UK: Scolar Press, 1994).
6. William Baldwin and Andrew Knapp, *The Newgate Calendar: Comprising Interesting Memoirs of the Most Notorious Characters Who Have Been Convicted of Outrages on the Laws of England since the Commencement of the Eighteenth Century, with Occasional Anecdotes and Observations, Speeches, Confessions, and Last Exclamations of Sufferers* (London: J. Robins, 1825).

CHAPTER 3: THE 1950S AND 1960S:
CARS AND THEME PARKS

1. Wade Sampson, "The Disneyland 1953 Sales Pitch," MousePlanet, accessed January 16, 2021, https://www.mouseplanet.com/9312/The_Disneyland_1953_Sales_Pitch.

2. Bob Thomas, *Walt Disney: An American Original* (Glendale, CA: Disney Editions, 2012).

CHAPTER 4: THE 1950S–1980S:
COMPUTERS TO ARCADES TO CONSOLES

1. Stewart Brand, "The First Intergalactic Space War Olympics," *Rolling Stone*, December 7, 1972.
2. Stewart Brand, *Whole Earth Catalog*, September 1, 1968.
3. Brand, "First Intergalactic."
4. Anna Weiner, "The Complicated Legacy of Stewart Brand's 'Whole Earth Catalog,'" *New Yorker*, November 16, 2018, https://www.newyorker.com/news/letter-from-silicon-valley/the-complicated-legacy-of-stewart-brands-whole-earth-catalog.
5. Chris Baker, "Stewart Brand Recalls First 'Spacewar' Video Game Tournament," *Rolling Stone*, May 25, 2016, https://www.rollingstone.com/culture/culture-news/stewart-brand-recalls-first-spacewar-video-game-tournament-187669/.
6. Brand, " First Intergalactic."
7. Phil Hoad, "Tetris: How We Made the Addictive Computer Game," *Guardian*, June 2, 2014, https://www.theguardian.com/culture/2014/jun/02/how-we-made-tetris.

CHAPTER 5: THE 1970S AND 1980S:
DUNGEONS & DRAGONS AND LARP

1. Lizzie Stark, *Leaving Mundania: Inside the Transformative World of Live Action Role-Playing Games* (Chicago: Chicago Review Press, 2012).

2. Jaakko Stenros and Markus Montola, *Nordic Larp* (Stockholm: Fea Livia, 2010).

CHAPTER 6: THE 1970S–1990S: A GAME VOCABULARY FOR THE PUBLIC

1. Patrick Smith, "The Extraordinary Story Of 'The Crystal Maze,' The Most Epic Game Show Ever Made," *BuzzFeed*, May 18, 2015, https://www.buzzfeed.com/patricksmith/to-the-crystal-dome.
2. N. R. Kleinfield, "Video Games Industry Comes Down to Earth," *New York Times*, October 17, 1983.
3. Edward Rothstein, "A New Art Form May Arise From the 'Myst,'" *New York Times*, December 4, 1994.
4. Emily Yoshida, "Lost to the Ages," *Grantland*, September 24, 2013, http://grantland.com/features/looking-back-game-myst-20th-anniversary/.

CHAPTER 7: THE 1980S–2020S: NEW WAYS OF LOOKING AT SHARED SPACES

1. Richard Formby, "Free festivals supplement from International Times c1974," Instagram @richard_formby, July 17, 2020, https://www.instagram.com/p/CCvS9xznGM2/.
2. Andy Roberts and Susan J. Blackmore, *Albion Dreaming: A Popular History of LSD in Britain (Revised Edition with a New Foreword by Dr. Sue Blackmore)* (Singapore: Marshall Cavendish Editions, 2008).
3. "Glastonbury Festival: Historical Overview," Internet Archive, June 30, 2008, https://web.archive.org/web/20080630095849/http://archive.glastonburyfestivals.co.uk/HISTORY/overview.html.

Notes

CHAPTER 8: THE 1990S–2000S:
THE DOT-COM ERA AND BEYOND

1. Edgar Allan Poe, "Secret Writing," *Graham's Magazine*, August 1841, https://www.eapoe.org/works/essays/gm41sw01.htm.
2. Bernard Weinraub, "'Blair Witch' Proclaimed First Internet Movie," *Chicago Tribune*, August 17, 1999, https://www.chicagotribune.com/news/ct-xpm-1999-08-17-9908170065-story.html.
3. Monty Phan, "Studios Turning to Elaborate Internet Games for Promotion," *Los Angeles Times*, July 13, 2001, https://www.latimes.com/archives/la-xpm-2001-jul-13-ca-21935-story.html.

CHAPTER 9: THE 2000S: PRECURSORS AND
THE BIRTH OF ESCAPE ROOMS

1. "Szimpla Kert," n.d., http://en.szimpla.hu/szimpla-garden.
2. Edan Corkill, "Real Escape Game Brings Its Creator's Wonderment to Life," *Japan Times*, December 20, 2009, https://www.japantimes.co.jp/life/2009/12/20/general/real-escape-game-brings-its-creators-wonderment-to-life/.
3. Ryoji Shimada, "What Is Real Escape Game? Originally from Japan," Manabink, October 10, 2020, https://manabink.com/en/2020/10/10/what-is-real-escape-game-originally-from-japan/.
4. Takao Kato, "Message from the President: SCRAP Corporate Philosophy," SCRAP, n.d., https://www.scrapmagazine.com/about/message/.

Notes

CHAPTER 10: THE 2010S TO NOW: THE RISE
OF ESCAPE ROOM GAMES

1. Lisa Spira, "US Escape Room Industry Report – 2020 Year End Update (February 2021)," Room Escape Artist, February 26, 2021, https://roomescapeartist.com/2021/02/26/us-escape-room -industry-report-2020-year-end-update-february-2021/.

CHAPTER 24: PADLOCKS AND OTHER
LOCKING MECHANISMS

1. Peter Caine, *The Definitive Guide to The Da Vinci Code: Paris Walks* (London: Orion, 2006).

CHAPTER 28: RED HERRINGS

1. Michael Quinion, "The Lure of the Red Herring," World Wide Words, n.d., http://www.worldwidewords.org/articles/herring.htm.